THE LIES THAT BIND

An Adoptee's Journey Through
Rejection, Redirection,
DNA, and Discovery

by Laureen Pittman

This edition published by Laureen Pittman via Amazon KDP
Text © Laureen Pittman 2018
ISBN-13: 978-1793142979

Edited and Formatted by: Angie Martin
Cover Design by: Amanda Walker

To learn more about author Laureen Pittman,
please visit her website at www.adoptionmytruth.com.

For Heide,
a generous soul,
who held the key
to me.

Foreword

Fate introduced me to Laureen Pittman. Or, maybe it was divine intervention. Something much larger than us connecting two souls who had flailed around in the same rocky waters of adoption. No matter how the two of us came together, it was meant to be, though neither of us would realize the extent of it for over a year.

There are many sides to adoption – not all of which are heard. Definitely not understood. Even those involved in it don't quite know how to process the intense emotions that go along with adoption. To further complicate matters, the stories of adoption are boundless. No two tales are the same. The experiences and emotions are so varied, it's impossible to capture them all. And, yet, there is a connection with those who have been caught up in the currents, tossed about, and searching for something to latch onto and steady us through the storms.

When I heard Laureen's story for the first time in a writer's group in San Bernardino, I saw a kindred spirit. I wasn't about to tell her that, though. See, Laureen was given up for adoption and was still struggling on her journey. I, on the other hand, had given up a child for adoption twenty years earlier – and I wasn't quite ready to admit it to anyone.

It wasn't the shame or embarrassment of having the child. No, it was the immense regret of my decision, one that has never settled in my soul. When I learned of my pregnancy, I knew I had no financial means of raising him. I even handpicked his adoptive parents after interviewing them… and they provided him with an incredible life. The one I wish I had been able to give him.

I was lucky in that I always knew where he was, what he was doing, and could follow his upbringing through letters, then later through Facebook. It didn't make it any easier, though. And, for the two years prior to meeting Laureen, I had desperately longed to get in touch with him, but I had yet to take the first steps to contact my son. If I could even call him that.

Adoption can tear a person apart, no matter where they fit into the story. But, the desperate need to experience belonging to a family doesn't end with the child. Some birthmothers feel that piece of them ripped away at relinquishment, and they never recover. I was – and still am – one of them.

Laureen's tale from the point of view of an adoptee is one of incredible bravery and courage. Throughout the search for her birthparents and the truth about her history, the message of acceptance and belonging is clear. The mystery, sentiments, and self-awareness found within these pages is something that will change lives. Her beautiful voice echoes through the pages with pain and joy, disappointment and redemption. No matter if you have been involved in adoption directly or not, there is beauty to be found in this heart-wrenching book.

I will never know what it would have been like had I made a different choice for my son. However, with newfound strength from Laureen's story, which you are about to read, I did contact him, meet him, and I have begun my own journey. *Our* journey. One that will continue to grow over the years.

And, I have Laureen to thank for that.

Angie Martin

Author's Note

The Lies That Bind is a memoir and work of creative nonfiction. The story is based on my memories growing up adopted and my journey as an adult to find and connect with my biological family.

Personal letters, e-mail, and government correspondence are reproduced in whole or in part, as written by the original authors, without correction. Any typos, grammatical errors, etc., belong to the original writer of the communication.

The graphics contained in Chapter 11 of this book have been recreated by me using original data presented and received from the website *23andMe.com*. The graphics are a derivative of the original graphics shown on the website and provided to me through my personal *23andme.com* account, for which I have ownership rights, and are meant to convey the data as originally received.

The narrative and any dialogue are faithful to my recollections. As a memoir about my adoption experience, the story is fragmented and missing pieces. Some of what I know as the truth may not be another person's truth.

In addition, this work also attempts to recreate, through investigation and imagination, certain key moments that affected my life, but for which I was not present. These bits of "fiction" are created based on dogged research and stories that have been told to me by people I trust.

Ersatz Life
(part one)
A poem by Laureen Pittman

Born for no reason; born to no one.
An unending sense of transience
No familiar face in sight.
Identity stunted, limited, inadequate
Shaped by ideas, myth, fractions
Of a history told by well-meaning Others.

The utter incompetence
of being.

A saga of secrecy and lies
Stories, justifications and rationalizations
Meant to pacify and soothe
The pain of unacknowledged
Trauma
But serve only to undermine
Truth
That lies in wait.

Prologue

It was written I should be loyal to the nightmare of my choice.
~Joseph Conrad, "Heart of Darkness"

December 15, 1963

Margaret ambled across the prison courtyard, acutely aware of the eyes focused on her swollen belly. She was not the type of person others might notice in any normal, everyday setting, say, just walking down the street. She was small in stature, plain but not unattractive, poised but unassuming in her habits and mannerisms. Here in this place, confined in more ways than one, she could not hide her distorted figure or the inconvenience it caused her. They watched. They whispered. She did her best to ignore them.

Unsteady, but with purpose, Margaret hastened her step. She focused her gaze on the open book in her hands, hoping the grimace on her face made her look like she was simply concentrating on a gripping story that might be unfolding on the pages in front of her. But, in reality, the book was just a prop. The heaviness and the pain in her abdomen were overwhelming, and she could no longer hide it.

It was still four weeks until her estimated due date, but her discomfort had become unbearable. The thing growing inside of her was pressing against her insides, jostling her bladder, stomach, and lungs for room to grow.

At eighteen, Margaret understood the physiology of her situation, but avoided, at all costs, the psychology of it. After all, the pregnancy was a temporary situation, just like the prison sentence.

No one in her family, not even her own mother, knew she was pregnant. In a strange twist of fortune, her conviction and incarceration allowed her to deal with the situation in the best way possible. She would handle it herself. No one who really mattered would need to know.

Margaret considered the pregnancy part of her punishment.

In 1963, the California Institute for Women was more like a structured commune than a prison. It was originally called "Frontera," a feminine derivative of the word frontier – a new beginning. At the time, CIW was California's only prison for female felons, including convicted murderers. The infamous Manson Girls were housed there on death row, although they would not arrive at the prison until shortly after Margaret's departure.

The prison's location in a rural, uninhabited area in southern California was expected to encourage the residents (the women were not referred to as inmates or prisoners) to view the institution as a self-contained community. The campus-like design of the prison grounds was in keeping with the progressive notion of rehabilitation at the time. There were no perimeter fences, no razor wire, no lookout towers, no visible armed guards roaming around. Residents were housed in single or double rooms in housing units or "cottages," each with its own courtyard, situated around a central campus.

The design of the prison was meant to foster a "free-world" feel. Staff and prisoners wore clothing that resembled street clothes rather than uniforms. Correctional supervisors were called "matrons" and were encouraged to develop "motherly" relationships with the residents in order to understand the individual needs of the women in their care. The goal was to establish individualized treatment programs for the women, depending on their rehabilitative needs.

Despite being subject to count three times a day, residents were allowed, for the most part, to move around the prison grounds with relative freedom. A typical schedule for a resident would include a minimum of four hours a day of work, at jobs necessary to maintain the prison, in the library, or at the on-site garment factory. Residents who were younger than fifty-five were also required to take homemaking classes. Training in cosmetology, laundry, sewing, and cooking was also available. High school courses were required for those who had not graduated from high school. The women were also required to participate in twice-weekly problem-solving sessions with their living groups in the cottages. Group and individual counseling were also available on a voluntary basis. Most of the matrons were trained in social work and deemed qualified to counsel the women.

Margaret was different than most of the younger girls. She had already received her high school diploma – graduated early, in fact – and was even attending the local community college to advance her knowledge and interest in politics and the law. She dreamed about going to law school. But now, stuck at Frontera and pregnant at eighteen, she endured the mindless work with which she was charged, as well as the homemaking classes, knowing it would only be a matter of time before she would be able to get her real life back again. Although she was sentenced to a ten-year prison term, she was counting on serving a much shorter sentence, as was the case with "well-behaved" residents.

Margaret was a good girl in prison. She kept to herself most of the time and read books from the library to keep herself connected with the outside world. Margaret tolerated the group problem-solving sessions, but insisted she didn't need any individual counseling, despite her situation. She was, however, required to meet with a *real* social worker on occasion. Someone from the outside. Someone whose primary concern was the *baby*, not Margaret. During these meetings, Margaret was forced to face reality. Forced to deal with the thing she was avoiding. The *pregnancy*. When speaking with the social worker, she told stories – even made stuff up – and talked about her *feelings*. It needed to make sense to the social worker, so Margaret played along.

The social worker did her job. From the file:

CASE SUMMARY: Birth mother was seen by the intake worker on November 1, 1963, at Frontera, where she was incarcerated for narcotics. She is an 18-year old high school graduate, pregnant and unmarried and not desiring marriage to the father of the baby. The birth mother requests adoption because she feels this would be the only plan for her to make for herself and for her child. She had plans of continuing with college. She is quite an intelligent girl, and the social worker feels that she has an excellent outlook.

Birth mother realizes the extent of her decision and does not feel that it was made without a great deal of thought. She seems to get along quite well at Frontera and has a very charming personality. She and the birth father have an intellectual relationship. She does not feel that she was truly in love with him and for this reason did not want to marry him. He did not know that she was pregnant for sure.

Margaret finally reached the cottage and pushed open the door. The book fell to the floor as she doubled over in pain. Two residents who were standing nearby rushed to her aid and helped her to her room, where she lay down on her bed. The pain and pressure subsided momentarily. Her eyes darted nervously around the room. She felt a warm gush between her legs. It was happening.

The matron arrived and hustled the other women out of the room. She pulled a chair from the corner of the room and positioned it close to the bed, facing Margaret as she lay on her side. The matron fixed her gaze on Margaret, but glanced at her watch each time Margaret flinched. Margaret turned away from the stout and stern authority figure and faced the wall. That's when the tears began.

"You don't need to look at me for me to tell whether you're having a contraction. I can tell. I gotta time 'em, so I'm just gonna sit here with you. No need to call the hospital just yet." The matron was unemotional. "Your baby's not supposed to come for three or four more weeks, but your water broke, so it's coming for sure."

Margaret continued to labor in her wet clothing, lying on the fluid-soaked cot for nearly two hours. The contractions were strong but far apart, and the matron, who consulted with the powers-that-be in the main building via walkie-talkie, didn't feel the need to rush Margaret to the hospital. Margaret moved as little as possible, facing the wall, determined not to give the matron the satisfaction of seeing the fear and pain in her eyes or the tears melting into her pillow.

By the time the medical transport team arrived at the cottage to take Margaret to the hospital for the delivery, she was crying out in pain. Some of the cottage residents had gathered at the door, hoping to get a glimpse of what was going on. Maybe she'd have the baby right there in the prison cottage.

The contractions were strong once Margaret arrived at the hospital. Inside, she was escorted, though made to walk on her own, to a stark, sterile room with one bed and given a gown to change into. Relieved to finally peel away her still-damp clothing, she climbed onto the bed and waited. It was cold. There was no blanket; only a sheet. She noticed the restraints hanging from the bed rails. *Those must be for crazy women, not for me,* Margaret thought. *Where in the hell would I go, anyway? Let's just get this over with.*

Margaret lost track of time. She labored alone on the bed for some time. She had no knowledge of breathing techniques. No one to hold her hand or soothe her nerves. Nothing to eat or drink. No nurse checking in on her. A single window on one wall faced an inside hallway, but Margaret could not see out of it. She was sure they were watching.

Margaret began feeling nauseous in between contractions. Finally, a nurse entered the room. The woman, looking all business in perfect white from head-to-toe, didn't even glance at Margaret as she crossed the room. With her back toward Margaret, she busied herself at a small table on the other side of the room. When the nurse finally turned to speak and started walking toward her, Margaret's eyes focused on the white origami crown atop her perfectly coiffed head.

There was no conversation, just curt instruction. Margaret was shaved and given an enema. She tried her best to mentally float away from the humiliating scene, but the pain from the contractions, now closer together, kept bringing her back to reality.

Then, came the needle. Margaret didn't protest. She was still awake when another nurse entered the room, lifted the rails on the bed, and attached the restraints to her wrists and ankles. By the time the nurses were wrapping her head in the gauze-like turban, she was unaware of her surroundings, blindly floating away in a drug-induced twilight dream.

Out of nowhere came a small, high-pitched, furious wail. Margaret was in a blurred but conscious state. Through the drug haze, she felt something soft, wet, and wriggling on her thighs. She had no idea how much time had passed. She tried to wipe the sweat from her brow with her hand, but the restraints attached to her wrists wouldn't allow it. She tried to close her legs. The restraints restricted her ankles.

There was a man in the room now – the doctor, Margaret presumed. He was holding a small bloody bundle. He glanced at Margaret for just a moment, but didn't say a word. He turned his attention back to the matter at hand. He studied the tiny wriggling mass of flesh, seemed satisfied with its frail, angry cries, and handed it to one of the nurses.

Margaret looked away. She closed her eyes and willed herself to be taken away from reality once again. She heard one of the nurses murmur, "It's a girl."

PART I: MARGARET

Chapter One – Baby Girl Michaels

A people without the knowledge of their past history,
origin and culture is like a tree without roots.
~Marcus Garvey

I was born Baby Girl Michaels. On the day of my birth, there was no celebration or joy. There was, I imagine, only fear and sorrow. And, perhaps, relief. Yes, I am sure there was relief. Part of the burden carried by the young woman who gave birth to me had finally been lifted.

I will never know the true story of my humble beginnings because the story of my birth has, for the most part, been a secret, considered a shameful thing that happened to *someone else* over fifty years ago. As an adoptee during the closed adoption era of the 1960s, I've been denied a very deep layer of my existence – no family history, no ethnicity, no heritage. But, here I am: existing, living life, and thriving, although some may argue about the thriving part. Some people still believe the past (*my* past) and history (*my* history) should be hidden and denied for all eternity in the name of "privacy" or to protect others from exposure to personal embarrassment, or to a truth that would destroy some perfectly-crafted life created out of secrecy, lies, and an outright denial of the past.

The adoption records are sealed. It was (and *still is*) the law in California. Like many young unwed mothers in the early 1960s, my birth mother was promised privacy and anonymity in exchange for choosing adoption. She was told to forget about *the baby* and move forward with her life. She was hopeful she would be able to walk away from that dark time in her life and, if she tried really hard, she could all but forget the whole experience (the drugs, the arrest, the conviction, prison, birth of a baby). She was, in her mind, allowed to be "reborn" as an adult and start a new life.

My birth mother served approximately four years of her ten-year prison sentence and was released into the world for her "do-over." By this time, I was a toddler, running around barefoot at home in San Bernardino, California. There was a period of several months between the time of my birth and the date I was placed with my adoptive family, during which I don't know where I was. Who cared for me during this crucial time? Was I held, rocked, soothed by a stranger's touch?

When I was finally placed with my adoptive parents in March of 1964, I came to them with full instructions, courtesy of the San Bernardino County Department of Social Services, Adoption Services:

Your baby was born December 15, 1963. She weighed 5 pounds 2.5 ounces and measured 17 inches. There were no delivery complications. She was one month premature.

Details about periodic exams by unnamed pediatricians were documented and provided to my parents. Apparently, I was in good health, despite a possibly drug-addicted mother and premature birth.

Your baby's day begins at 5:30 or 6:00 am. At this time, she is offered her first bottle of the day, after this, she will nap off and on through the morning.

A feeding schedule and care instructions were also provided.

At 1:00 pm your baby receives her bath. She does not particularly enjoy her bath and may cry for a time after being bathed and dressed.

Afternoon naps are flexible. Between 10:00 and 11:00 pm your baby is offered the last bottle for the day and goes to bed; she should then sleep through the night. Baby does not sleep well on her back.

I still don't sleep well on my back. I'm a tummy sleeper.

My adoptive parents, Henry and Lilouise (known as Hank and Little by their friends and family) were, by all accounts, doting parents. I even had a big brother. Hank and Little had adopted a baby boy two years before I entered their lives. Tommy had red hair, green eyes, and freckles. I was a brunette with brown eyes, like Hank and Little. I was often told I looked like Little. I thought that was funny because I knew I was adopted, but it made me feel warm and fuzzy anyway.

Little was a stay-at-home mom, and she did her best to do what she was supposed to do – raise her kids. I give my parents credit for making every effort to mold us into what they considered a conventional, stereotypical middle-class family in the 1960s and 70s.

Hank worked at the telephone company. I don't know exactly what he did there. Early on, I know he climbed telephone poles and installed telephone lines all across the Southern California Desert. During the time he worked in the desert, he brought home two desert tortoises we kept as pets. We named them both Oscar. At that time, we had the most unusual pets on the block.

A couple of years after my dad brought home the second Oscar, I was rolling my bike across the back patio and nearly stepped on a teeny tiny baby tortoise. I stopped in my tracks. I think I even screamed a little because it was such a startling sight. Our two original Oscars were huge – larger than my head. It seemed unreal to see a tiny cartoon version of those dinosaur-looking creatures we'd become accustomed to seeing hunkering across the lawn. Stunned, I called out for my mom.

My mom brought the tiny creature into the house and settled him into an old aquarium with some pebbles and rocks in it. She said she didn't even know the Oscars had laid any eggs. *Eggs?* Weird. My mom and I returned to the backyard and searched and searched for more mini Oscars, thinking there had to be more than just one, but we never found any others. I named him (her?) Tuxedo.

The poor little thing never seemed to thrive in that aquarium. My mom was determined, however. She would feed him all kinds of raw veggies he'd push around the aquarium and into the pebbles, mouth gaping wide open, trying to get a bite. She even fed him canned dog food for protein with calcium powder sprinkled on top that she bought at the pet store.

I felt sad for Tuxedo. Despite my mom's efforts with the protein and calcium powder, his shell was always too soft, he looked lonely, and he never had anywhere to go in that little aquarium. There were no other little Tuxedos to play with. Didn't he want to be near his mommy and daddy? The two big Oscars were still living outside, although they would hibernate under the tool shed during the winter. Little Tuxedo just seemed so out of place in the aquarium. More than once, I thought about taking Tuxedo outside to be with the Oscars. But, I never did. My mom had adopted him.

I don't remember exactly when Tuxedo died. One day, his aquarium was just gone.

Our normal-*ish* family went on vacations together during the winter, sometimes camping in our funky, cramped, pop-up tent-trailer. We visited all the usual spots in the West: The Grand Canyon, the Colorado River, Yosemite, the Giant Sequoias. There were lots of family road trips in my Dad's old truck. Back then, we were allowed to sit in the bed of the truck, which was covered with a camper shell that protected us from the elements. It wasn't particularly comfortable, but I preferred being there in the back rather than being up front with my parents because they were both dedicated chain smokers.

I hated everything about the cigarettes and smoking. I hated the way the smoke made my hair and clothes smell. I hated the click of the butane lighter. I hated the filthy ashtrays filled with disgusting cigarette butts, some with smudgy lipstick "kisses" on the filter. In the 60s and 70s, no one worried about the health effects of secondhand smoke (hell, no one worried about first-hand smoke, either).

In addition to the smoking, there was a lot of drinking. It didn't occur to me until I was in my twenties and had left home to live on my own that maybe my mother was an alcoholic. When my brother and I were young, my father would have a cocktail almost every night when he got home from work. Then, he'd have a cup of coffee after dinner. I remember my mother, however, climbing on the step stool in the kitchen in the hours before my father got home, reaching up to the top shelf to grab the big jug of generic vodka. She'd stand on the stool and pour herself a hefty glass – straight up – then climb down and move the stool back to its resting place in the corner on the other side of the kitchen.

I don't know how often she did this throughout the day (perhaps even before my brother and I got home from school?), but it explained the afternoon naps. Other moms weren't napping the afternoon away. My best friend Debbie's mom worked full-time. My other best friend Nancy's mom was going to law school. Despite their busy lives, both moms showed up on occasion to watch our softball games and swim meets. Not my mom.

Back then, I didn't wonder too much about why my mom didn't have the time to go shopping with me or come watch me pitch in the game. I assumed she just wasn't interested. Once in school, I think I was in the second or third grade at the time, I had a terrible sore throat that just kept getting worse as the day dragged on. My teacher sent me to the office. The office secretary called my mother to tell her I was ill and needed to go home. When the secretary hung up, she asked me if I was okay to walk home. I told her I was. I just assumed my mom was too busy (again) to come and pick me up. Or, maybe she didn't understand how much my throat hurt. I walked the mile home in the middle of the day, spitting every thirty feet or so because it was too painful to swallow. I walked to and from school every day, so it really didn't seem like a big deal at the time. I look back now and think, *What in the hell was my mom doing that she couldn't drive eight blocks to school and pick me up in the middle of the day?*

My mother and I were never close. I didn't feel affected by the distance between us when I was younger. I just spent less time at home and more time with my friends. I sort of "adopted" Debbie's mom, Betty, as a second mother, and enjoyed her presence and encouragement. I knew our families were different, but the only difference I could figure out was that my brother and I were adopted, and Debbie and her sister were not. Maybe, if I was my mom's *real* daughter, she would have treated me differently. More like how the *real* moms I knew treated their *real* daughters.

In my early teens, I remember once searching through the house for my mom to ask her about something – probably to ask if it was okay to go to Debbie's house for dinner or to spend the night. I couldn't find her in the house, so I went out to the "back forty," where my parents parked the travel trailer (a step up from the old pop-up tent trailer) in between road trips. Sure enough, Mom was in there. Alone. I could smell the cigarette smoke as I approached the door. She was probably busy cleaning and getting ready for their next trip. Once my brother and I were in our teens, Mom and Dad would take off for the entire winter, bound for the Trinity River up near the California-Oregon border. It was their escape from the monotony of everyday life. Perhaps it was their escape from Tommy and me.

I swung open the door and climbed in. There she was, sitting at the table that turned into a bed, crying. She stood up quickly and tried to look busy, dragging heavily on her cigarette.

"Mom, what's wrong?"

"Nothing… really."

"But, you've been crying."

"It's just…" She took another long drag on her cigarette.

"It's just that I always thought that if I had a daughter, we'd be *friends*."

I froze. Was she talking about *me*? She didn't *have* me – like give birth to me – but I *was* her daughter. Or, was she saying if she had had a *real* daughter, they'd be friends, but we can't actually *be* friends because I'm not *really* her daughter?

"We *are*!"

I blurted it out, but I didn't mean it. I didn't *feel* like her friend. I wasn't even sure whether I felt like her daughter. Was I doing it wrong? How were daughters supposed to feel or act? We never did any of the mother-daughter stuff my friends did with their moms.

As I stood there, dumbfounded, I had a vague sense that maybe I should hug my mother, but she was already turned around, busy rearranging paper plates and potholders in a cupboard above the table, cigarette dangling from the corner of her mouth. As I watched her, I tried to remember the last time we had hugged. I had never seen my mother cry before, either, and it was getting awkward. I didn't know what to do or say. I just wanted her to stop crying, and I wanted to get the hell out of there. I wanted to get over to Debbie's house and spend time with a *real* family.

She took another drag on her cigarette and then turned to me, expectantly. We hugged stiffly and muttered words that were meant to promise that we'd try to be friends in the future. Under the stale, musty scent of the cigarettes attached to her clothes, I smelled the vodka.

We never spoke of the incident in the trailer. And, we never really became friends.

15

Chapter Two – A Happy Childhood

A happy childhood...
is the worst possible preparation for life.
~Kinky Friedman

I didn't realize the dysfunction in my own family because I was too busy trying to be a *normal* kid. Normal for me meant trying to be like the other families. The *real* families. My brother and I spent loads of time outdoors after school and during the hot summer months running up and down the block with neighborhood friends. Our neighborhood was full of real families.

There were two mean brothers who lived up the street. They liked to hide behind bushes and throw rocks, acorns, and kumquats (or whatever else they could find) at me and my friends as we rode by on our bikes. There was a single working mother who lived across the street. She was raising three young kids on her own. Those were the first "latchkey kids" I ever knew. When they came home from school, one of the older neighborhood girls from up the street would come down to their house to make bologna sandwiches for them and keep an eye on them until their mother returned home from work. I didn't realize until I was a mother myself what a real champion this mom was and how lucky her kids were to have such a strong woman as a role model during a difficult time.

Across the street, on the corner to the left, lived another woman with three children. She was a single mother for a little while, as well, but I don't really remember that period of time. Her first husband – the father of her children – died when the kids were young, and she remarried fairly quickly. I'm not sure how those kids felt about their stepfather, but we thought he was a riot. I remember my mother standing at the kitchen window, watching the "show" almost every evening. Sometimes, Dan's car would jump the curb halfway up the block before coming to a sloppy stop in front of his house. It was always entertaining watching Dan get out of the car, swaying to get his balance, then stumble up the curb toward the walkway. My mother would stand at the kitchen window before my father got home, chain-smoking her Raleigh cigarettes, often having a cocktail herself (her usual straight-up cheap vodka), and giving my brother and me the play-by-play of Dan's arrival.

"Only one tire up on the curb today."

Would he make it up the walk and to the steps of the porch before falling? Or, would he just give up and take a booze nap somewhere in the unkempt, ankle-deep grass until his wife, Jan, came home and helped him to the door? It was comedy. I suppose I should say that I *thought* it was comedy, until I realized when I was older how tragic it really was. He was a school teacher, for Christ's sake. Apparently, he would stop at the Red Fox (a local dive bar that had a huge sign out front with a picture of a cartoon fox wearing a top hat, smoking a pipe, and holding a martini) after wrangling with fifth graders all day and pickle himself nearly unconscious. Then, he would drive himself home about three miles every day.

They may have been *real* families, but there was no shortage of dysfunction in our neighborhood. I think the obvious differences I perceived in other families around the neighborhood made me feel secure in thinking that my family was *normal*. We may not be *real*, but at least we're *normal*.

Middle school ("junior high," we called it back then) for me was without much drama and fairly uneventful. I got through it by concentrating on my schoolwork – I didn't even *try* to fit in. Being cool and part of the "in crowd" wasn't my thing. I was happy to simply broker the notes between my two good looking and popular best friends and the boys who liked them. Boys would call me on occasion, but it was either to talk about a homework assignment or to find out whether Nancy or Debbie was available for a make-out session after school under the freeway overpass. They both wore real bras in the seventh grade. I didn't even need a training bra until the ninth grade.

High school was a good time. I kept my grades up (graduated salutatorian), participated in student government (managed to get elected senior class president), and found myself in the middle of normal teenage mischief (there's that word again: *normal*). More of a nerd than a cool kid, my friends and I would occasionally ditch an early class to grab breakfast and bring back donuts for the vice principal and some of the teachers we liked. We even had a hand in vandalizing the rival high school's property before the big game (it was an annual tradition to paint the big "P" at Pacific High School with our own school colors of red and black). By the time I was a junior, I was sneaking out of my bedroom window in the middle of the night to drink a few beers and hang out with friends.

I was so busy trying to be a normal kid that I hardly ever thought about being adopted.

What *is* normal, anyway? Normal is what you *know*. Of course, I can look back now and clearly see the dysfunction of my family, as well as the insecurities I may have harbored and my attempts to find validation from outside sources. In my mind, however, it had nothing to do with my brother and me being adopted. On the surface, we were no different than most other families.

College, on the other hand, was a different kind of struggle. I was the first person in my immediate family to pursue a degree at a four-year university. My brother had ventured into the military – first the Marines and then the Navy. He flopped around between services, got married,

18

started a family at age twenty-two, and eventually found gainful employment at the local grocery store. As for my desire to go to college, my parents were unprepared to pay for my education or to take on any debt on my behalf, so I lived at home and enrolled at the local state college, working twenty to thirty hours a week at Sears and Longs Drug Store to pay for tuition. I commuted from home to work and school. My parents helped out where they could with expenses for things like books and gas money. They were proud of me, but more than a little perplexed by my ambition. I was a little perplexed by my ambition, as well. I knew I wanted to do something important with my life, but I didn't know what – or how to go about figuring it out.

Eventually, I was able to get a student job at an office on campus, allowing me to spend *a lot* of time at school. I basically only slept at home, which was fine with me. I worked during the day and went to classes at night. Any free time was spent at the campus either in the library studying or in the Pub in the student union building, hanging out with friends.

The Pub was a popular place – it was the only place on campus that served alcohol. Back in the 1980s, it was easy to alter a driver's license with an aspirin and a sharp pencil. Everyone did it. My date of birth, according to my California Driver's License was 12-15-1960, not 12-15-1963. Not only did it work at the Pub, but at the clubs and bars around town.

Besides work and school, I found time for drinking and partying. I prided myself in being able to knock back quite a few drinks and still make it to work or class the next day. Weekends always included drinking and sometimes a little marijuana or cocaine. I don't remember ever paying for the drugs, but it was easy to get, as long as you were hanging out with the right people.

I had a regular boyfriend – the same guy I'd been dating since I was a sophomore in high school. He was two years older than me and was not in college. He worked nights at a local mini market. We dated off and on for years, but we both led separate lives, even dating other people. I don't know why we didn't just break up after we graduated from high school – I look back now and think it might possibly have been my need for some sort of security. For him, the answer was easy: I was always available, if you know what I mean.

I had another on-and-off boyfriend who had a much older sister who managed a liquor store. So, early on, even before we graduated from high school, as long as we had money (all my friends had jobs at age sixteen), we had access to all the beer, Bartles & Jaymes, and Boone's Farm we could handle.

I know I went a little crazy during the 1980s. I had already lost my virginity without much fanfare in high school. The drinking made it easier. Casual sex was just that: casual sex. No big deal. It would still be a few years before anyone was concerned about HIV/AIDS, so I was tallying up the trysts without a care in the world. Feeling smart and empowered. In control.

It was a perfect environment. I didn't *think* I had issues with sensitivity to rejection and abandonment, but in hindsight, I realize I did (and maybe still do) have difficulty allowing myself to be emotionally vulnerable. Most young people don't have the capacity for real sustained intimacy, but add on the unfinished and unacknowledged struggle with identity, trust, and a never-ending search for affirmation and acceptance that many adoptees feel, and you've got a great breeding ground for destructive behavior. Casual sex was the perfect way for me to feel in control and avoid rejection.

It's clear to me now that from my late teens through my mid-twenties, sex for me was detached from any kind of emotional commitment. I struggled with the difference between genuine pleasure associated with intimacy and the fleeting high and exhilaration of feeling wanted and desired. My girlfriends were confused about how I could just jump from relationship to relationship, or partner to partner, without any kind of attachment. I didn't need to *fall in love*. I didn't want to. They said I was like a man in that way. All I know is that I was in control. It felt good to not get involved emotionally. I used to be so perplexed by my friends crying over their boyfriends who dumped them. Who needed that kind of drama? Pass me another wine cooler.

My parents never asked any questions. I guess they figured as long as I kept my grades up, paid my bills, and came home at some point each night (or early morning), everything was fine. I know there were some mornings when they had to realize something was amiss. But, they never asked me to explain those early morning trips to the bathroom to throw up or trudging into the kitchen to gobble handfuls of aspirin.

Chapter Three – Family Ties

The bond that links your true family is not one of blood,
but of respect and joy in each other's life.
~Richard Bach

College was a wild time, for sure, but I still worked hard. Most of my friends who took the college route had left home to attend a four-year college or university. They lived in the dorms or off campus with other students and got to experience *real* independence. Stuck at home, I felt like I was missing out.

For three years I toiled away, living at home with my parents, working part-time and going to college. Desperate to spread my wings, I wanted to add some interest and excitement to my final year.

I didn't have to search long for the solution to my restlessness. The California State University system had (and still has) an International Program that affords students the opportunity to study abroad. Honestly, though, I was thinking less about the academic opportunity and cultural experience and more about the opportunity to finally get out of the house and live the real college life independent of my parents, like many of my friends were doing.

Even though I had four years of French language under my belt (two in high school and two in college), I decided to make it easier on myself by applying for a program in the United Kingdom. Without a language barrier, studying and communicating with the locals would be much easier. There were several universities in England that offered programs in political studies (I was majoring in political science), so I filled out the application and crossed my fingers.

There was a selection process. I don't remember exactly what the minimum requirements were, but I had a decent grade point average, and I was confident of the essay I wrote explaining why I wanted to study politics abroad in the middle of the soon-to-be-doomed *Cold War.* I'm fairly certain I didn't disclose my desire to party in a foreign country and meet guys with sexy British accents. There were only a few slots to fill, so I waited on pins and needles to hear the news.

I was over the moon when I received the acceptance letter. I was headed to the University of Bradford in West Yorkshire, England for my senior year. I had no idea where Bradford or West Yorkshire was, but it didn't matter. I had never even been on a plane until I was eighteen years old. Now, I was barely twenty and leaving the country to live in a foreign land (and go to school) for nearly an entire year.

Mom and Dad weren't at all surprised I had been selected, but my mom flipped out when she learned that I was headed to *Bradford, England*, of all places. She couldn't believe it. As it turned out, my adoptive mother's family is actually *from* Bradford. Her mother and aunt came to the United States from England in the early 1900s and eventually settled in southern California. I didn't know that. What were the odds? Of all the places in the entire world her family could have been from, they were from Bradford, England.

That was all my mother could talk about: *Bradford, Bradford, Bradford.* She was so excited for me to travel across "The Pond" to spend time in the place where half of our family originated. Wide-eyed, she started digging out old photos and documents.

"You must find the *Varleys!*"

Mom dug out old black and white photos, creased documents, and weathered postcards she had stored away in a hidden corner of the attic. Even though she had never been to England herself, she regaled me with stories of Bradford and how her mother and aunt came to this country on their own when they were just teenagers. She even unearthed a handwritten record of birth for Samuel Varley born in Bradford in 1859. I was impressed with the age of this document – the frayed, yellowed paper – and the fact that the information was handwritten in a weird, formal cursive style where the letter "s" looked like an "f." But frankly, I didn't know who Samuel Varley was. Nor did I care.

Seriously, I did *not* care about the Varleys. I was twenty years old and on my way to an exciting new land to have the adventure of a lifetime! And besides, the Varleys weren't *my* relatives. They were *her* relatives.

This was the first time in a long time I had thought about being adopted. Was it because I was adopted that I just didn't care about these Varley people? Or, was it because I was a twenty-year-old, self-absorbed girl who couldn't wait to flaunt her newfound independence (and try some well-hopped ale in a real British pub)?

The Varleys didn't mean anything to me. Should I have felt guilty about that? When my brother and I were young, we didn't spend much time with extended family. Family holidays were usually just our little nuclear family – my parents and my brother and me – sitting around in the rarely used formal dining room eating off the good china. All my grandparents had died before I hit double digits in age, and we did not live close to any aunts, uncles, or cousins. *Family* just wasn't a word with much significance for me. I had no interest in the Varleys or in any other so-called *family*. I just wanted to get out of there and start living my new life.

The winter after my junior year came and went in a blur. I could think of nothing other than my big trip abroad. My *Grand Tour*, if you will.

Once situated in student housing in Jolly Ol' England, I wasted no time getting acquainted with the local pubs. I also met some fine proper Brits, drank tea with milk, ate some formidable curries, and did a little studying and traveling, of course. Everything was quite *tickety-boo.*

After a while (and some long-distance prodding from my mother), I managed to work up the enthusiasm to look into the Varley situation. While on a visit to the local post office in Bradford to mail some letters, I took the time to look up the name Varley in the local directory.

Bloody hell! I was overwhelmed to find pages and pages of Varleys in the Bradford directory. What in the world was I supposed to do with this information? This was 1985 in a small Yorkshire town – I had no way to refine or narrow down these results. For a second, I thought about ripping out the pages of the directory and shoving them in my coat pocket so I could air mail them to my mother and let her deal with the Varleys, but I didn't.

I eventually spoke to my mother on the phone. I had an arrangement with my parents to call every other week. Of course, there were no cell phones, but our student row house on Merton Road had a telephone in the basement we shared with the house next door. Not exactly what I would call a convenient situation – sharing a telephone with eleven other female college students from all over the world – but better than having to go into town and use a pay phone.

"Mom, there are literally *hundreds* of Varleys in Bradford. I'm not kidding! Pages and pages in the phone book. Now what?"

"Pages and pages? Still living in Bradford? Wow."

That was the end of that. Even when my parents came to Bradford to visit in the spring, the Varley situation didn't come up. I think my mother was just as overwhelmed as I was.

The whole Varley situation wasn't a total bust. It did get me thinking about my adoption. And, I kept thinking about it. I am not sure why the curiosity took hold so fervently while I was away that year in Bradford, but the urge to connect with my past became overwhelming. Growing up, I was conditioned to believe that being adopted was irrelevant. My adoptive family was my family, and that was the end of it. It made no sense to wonder or to question otherwise. But, now that I was removed from my adoptive family and out on my own (thousands of miles away), I began to recognize and explore how adoption had shaped me. I wanted to find the missing pieces of the puzzle – my puzzle. Where did I come from? Did I have a long-lost family like the Varleys?

I wrote to my parents during that year, expressing my desire to find my birth parents. They were surprised, but supportive in their response. Of course, I wasn't there when they read my letter, and who knows what they discussed amongst themselves about my desire to know more about my birth family. But, if they were worried, hurt, or against it for any reason, they kept it to themselves.

While I was still in England, I also wrote to a private investigation company called Worldwide Tracers, which specialized in adoption cases. They responded.

We would be thrilled to find your birth parents for you when you get back to the U.S. And we WILL find them.

My search would be a priority when I returned home. I would find my birth parents.

Chapter Four – The First Pieces of the Puzzle

*The seeker embarks on a journey to find what he wants
and discovers, along the way, what he needs.*
~Wally Lamb

I returned home from the United Kingdom in the winter of 1986. Still in need of a few more units for graduation, I enrolled once again at my hometown campus. I went back to my office job on campus, so again, I was spending quite a bit of time at the university while still living at home with my parents.

I was *home*, but something felt different. Then, I remembered.

Hiraeth is a Welsh word meaning a homesickness for a home or a place to which you cannot return, somewhere that perhaps never was; nostalgia, yearning or grief for the lost places of one's past. The first time I had heard it was when I was studying in England.

During a break from my studies at the local pub (or, were the studies really just a break from the pubs?), I was asked by a friend, Carys, a sweet girl from Wales, if I had been homesick at all while I was in Bradford.

I thought about it for a moment. I was having a great time – a wonderful adventure in a new land – studying, playing, enjoying my independence, and for the first time, learning about myself as an individual and how to live and be something other than what my parents (or anyone else) expected of me. And, all the boys had dreamy accents.

"No way!" Perhaps my answer was a little too enthusiastic.

As we sat there, sipping our pints, I sensed that Carys didn't feel quite the same way. I asked her if she was homesick. Her home in Wales was over two hundred and fifty miles away from the green dales of West Yorkshire. After a thoughtful moment, she told me it wasn't really a homesickness she felt. She tried to explain.

Yes, Carys missed her home, her parents, and her dog. She also missed her best friend, who was at university in Ireland. She knew all of that (the people, the dog, the places) would be there when she returned, but she knew that returning home to Wales would not cure the sense of melancholy she felt for the careless days of her youth. She would return as an *adult*. It would all be different, including the expectations put upon her not just by everyone else, but by her own ambitions.

I thought she was feeling distressed about the realities of growing up. But, it was more than that. I didn't really grasp it until months later when I was back home.

Hiraeth is an unattainable longing for a place, a time, a person or people; a history that no longer exists or may never have actually existed at all. To feel *hiraeth* is to feel a deep incompleteness and yet recognize it as familiar.

After my year abroad, I felt consumed with a peculiar sense of urgency for something I could not identify that would not allow me to relax and get on with my life. I felt stuck, but at the same time, propelled forward. There was something left undone within me.

Was I was compelled by *hiraeth* to uncover my secrets? Maybe I had a little Welsh in me.

I became determined to find my birth parents – or at least learn as much as I could about my biological family. I was off to a good start. Hank and Little were, indeed, supportive and gave me the adoption paperwork they had saved all those years that bore my birth mother's last name. I kept hearing over and over about sealed records, but it never occurred to me my adoptive parents might have kept copies of the actual court filings. I'm glad mine did. I had the first piece of the puzzle: *"In the Matter of the Adoption of Baby Girl Michaels."*

I had a great piece of information to start my search: my birth mother's last name. But, this was 1986. Hardly anyone owned a personal computer. The World Wide Web was in its infancy; it wasn't the research and information powerhouse that it is today. And, all I had was a last name – a fairly common last name.

While finishing up my degree in political science, I was also taking courses to complete my certificate in paralegal studies. In my family law class, I focused on adoption research and wrote several papers on the subject. Thanks to all that research, I knew I had a right to receive non-identifying information from my file stored with the San Bernardino County Welfare Services.

I also knew the State of California had a mutual consent system that could be helpful in my search. Mutual consent systems or adoption registries were being used by many states to facilitate and coordinate the execution and recording of privacy waivers that are required for the potential release of identifying information. The systems allowed individuals directly involved in adoptions to indicate their willingness (or unwillingness) to have their identifying information disclosed to blood relatives (usually parents or siblings) who may be looking for them. In California, the consent of at least one birth parent and an adopted person over the age of eighteen is needed to release identifying information. Consent is given by filing an executed affidavit with the appropriate authority (in my case, the County of San Bernardino) consenting to the release of personal information. Sounds straightforward, doesn't it?

The mutual consent and waiver system still exists in California and in many other states. With the advancement of technology, the evolution of the Internet, and the burgeoning databases, a growing number of private registries have also popped up, many of which have proven to be successful search tools for adoptees and birth parents. Some charge a fee to register, some do not.

I looked into how to best register with the information I had. I thought I should at least sign a Waiver of Rights to Confidentiality, which documented my consent to allow my personal information to be shared. Such a waiver would be in my file at the county where my adoption was facilitated on the chance someone in my birth family was looking for me.

I called the San Bernardino County Department of Social Services. I spoke to a very nice gentleman named Bill Witt. I explained my situation and made an appointment to meet with him and sign a waiver.

I don't remember everything Mr. Witt and I talked about on the phone, but I do remember he asked me to bring a recent photograph of myself so he would have it on file in case he had contact from any of my biological family members. I remember nervously thinking, *Maybe, he knows something. Maybe, there is already a waiver on file from my birth mother! Why else would he ask me to bring a photo?* I had a weird feeling in my gut. Was it really going to be that easy? How exciting! How scary.

A few days later, I went to the San Bernardino County Social Services Department to meet with Mr. Witt. I signed the waiver. I gave him the photo – all big hair and bright Hawaiian-print blouse. Then, he handed me an official-looking envelope and told me he'd be in touch.

Huh? He'd be in touch for what? If my birth mother had already signed a waiver and it was in my file, wouldn't he be able to just tell me right then and there? Confusion set in. If there was no waiver, surely he wouldn't search for my birth mother. Why would he do that? In fact, the language of the waiver confirmed:

… the signing of this waiver does not necessarily insure that a contact can be arranged… the law prohibits the Department or agency from soliciting, directly or indirectly, the execution of… a waiver.

If there was no waiver from my birth mother already in my file, I figured I'd just sign my own waiver and it would get thrown in my super-secret file somewhere in the basement of the Social Services Department until (or if) my birth mother (or someone… maybe I had a sister!) decided to sign a waiver. What if she didn't know about the registry? Or worse, what if she didn't *want* contact from me?

I walked back to my car in a bit of a daze, grasping the envelope. *The envelope.* What could possibly be in the envelope? Once sitting in the car, I took a deep breath and opened it.

It was obvious Mr. Witt was familiar with my super-secret file. Apparently, after we spoke on the phone a few days earlier, he dug out my file to check out my story. And apparently, there was no waiver signed by my birth mother or by anyone else. But, Mr. Witt didn't stop there. He obviously read my file. Every last detail. The document in the envelope contained my non-identifying information – *in painstaking detail* – beautifully written on three pages of County Adoption Service official letterhead.

I was stunned. Not just by the information he provided, but by the fact he had gone to the trouble to tell me this story in such beautiful detail. It was beautiful to *me*, anyway. I don't even remember asking for non-identifying information – I just wanted to sign a waiver and see if my birth mother (or anyone else) had already signed one. I thought the information I had already received from my adoptive parents would be better than any dull non-identifying information he might be able to give me. After all, I had her *last name* on the legal adoption papers.

I was wrong.

I read the story. *My story.* I read it over and over. Sordid as it was, it was fascinating. And, it was *my* story. At the bottom of page three, Mr. Witt wrote:

"Laureen, I have begun to search for your birth family. The trail, however, is 23 years old so it may take some time. I'll keep you abreast of my progress."

He was going to *help* me?

At the time, I thought Bill Witt had gone way above and beyond the call of duty in the way he provided the non-identifying information to me. I was grateful I had found him when I did. I wondered about other adoptees (in California and across the country) who had been provided with their non-identifying information. Did they receive a story? Did they receive vivid detail about family members' hair color, skin tone, height, ambitions, and personality quirks? I had imagined the non-identifying information would be just some sort of factual outline or controlled listing of basic data.

Thank you, Bill Witt, for putting together my story.

County Adoption Service
San Bernardino County Department of Public Social Services
Serving the Adoption Triad

August 5, 1986

Dear Laureen:

I've had an opportunity to read your birth mother's file, and the following information may be helpful in answering some of your questions about your birth family background.

Your birth mother was born in Chicago, Illinois in 1945. Her ethnic background is English, French and Irish. At her first contact with the Agency, the social worker felt she might have had some Mexican or Hispanic background because she had an olive complexion, although medium light. Apparently, the olive skin derives from the French influence and is evident in several of her family members as well.

Your birth mother has a slender, heart-shaped face with nice features, and an unusually attractive nose with a rather broad, high bridge. She is slender (115 pounds), and has less than average bone structure for her height (5' 3 1/2"). She has long, dark hair and brown eyes.

Your birth mother is quiet, but too well poised to be shy. She is intelligent, converses well, and is frank about herself.

Your birth mother was quite interested in completing her education.

She spoke about becoming an attorney. She was also interested in mathematics, political science and enjoyed reading, particularly the Russian novelist, Dostoyevsky. In high school, your birth mother belonged to the Spanish Club and Girl's Athletic Association. She attended a summer session of a business college after graduation from high school.

Your birth mother does not remember her real father, as her parents separated when she was an infant. Her mother remarried when she was five years old. The only thing she remembered about her father was that he had dark hair. She has been very happy with her stepfather, feeling he was all things a father should be. Joe, as he is called, was a news editor and commentator. Joe had three years of college plus a technical school education.

Your birth maternal grandmother, Elle, was 36 years old at your birth. She was a very attractive woman – about 5' 8" tall, and slender at 120 pounds. Her hair was reddish-brown, light skin, rather ivory toned, with hazel eyes.

Your grandmother had a high school education and was a model for many years. She was also interested in singing and acting.

Your birth mother has four half siblings, the youngest three months old at your birth. Colleen was eleven at your birth. She is blonde, very fair, large bone structure, tall in stature. Colleen has hazel eyes and is very attractive. She is talented in dancing.

Joannie is nine years old, tall and slim with blue eyes, light skin and freckles.

Kenny is five. He is tall and slender with broad shoulders, fair skin, sandy-blonde hair, and hazel-blue eyes.

Baby Christian is the three-month-old half brother. He has dark hair.

Your birth father was born about 1943. He is Caucasian. His ethnic background is unknown. He is 5' 6" in height with a medium build. His skin is fair, eyes green and hair light brown.

In high school, your birth father was the editor of a literary magazine. He was also on the debating team and participated in political groups.

Your birth father is said to have a good sense of humor and gets along well with other people. He and your birth mother enjoyed talking about literature, intellectual subjects and attended classes together at the city college in their community. His plans after college are to teach at the junior college level.

Little information is available about your paternal grandparents. Your grandfather died about 1953 following an illness. Your grandmother has the same skin coloring as your birth father, perhaps a little lighter. She was described as stout, matronly, active and a scatterbrain. She never had to work and gadded about in her Mercedes automobile. Apparently, your birth father had no siblings.

Laureen, as you are aware, your birth mother was incarcerated for possession and use of drugs. In her interview with the social worker prior to your birth, she explained how she first became introduced to drugs. Your birth mother's parents met some people at a jazz concert and invited them to their home. The new acquaintances began coming over regularly, to the annoyance of your birth mother's stepfather. His wife, though, continued seeing them and included your birth mother in group activities such as smoking marijuana. Your birth mother felt flattered by the attention of her mother's friends and enjoyed the acceptance accorded her. I guess you might say your birth mother enjoyed the new "beatnik" culture, as it was called during that time period.

Your grandmother disassociated herself with this group, but your birth mother did not. She continued smoking pot, moved to San Francisco for a while, and then returned to her parents' home to finish high school. In her senior year, she had accumulated enough credits to attend only four hours of school daily; thus enabling her to attend classes at the local junior college with your birth father.

Your birth mother felt that she was responsible for getting your birth father started on narcotic drugs.

Both of your birth parents were arrested on drug-related charges. Your birth mother was sentenced to prison for ten years. She entered the California Institute for Women in September 1963, and was discharged in March 1967, after serving three years and six months. We have no record of your birth father following his arrest.

Laureen, the case notes summarizing your birth and your birth mother's situation reflect a great deal of insight and decisiveness and I would like to quote them verbatim as much as possible:

"Baby Girl _____ was born December 15, 1963, at CIW, Frontera, California. She was one month premature but

was in good condition at birth. She weighed 5 lbs 2 ½ oz.

The birth mother is firm in her decision to relinquish. She said she had wavered a couple of times but realized that adoption would be a better plan for the baby. She was in very high spirits and was anxious to get out of the hospital. She had been reading two books and planned to trade them with a nurse's aide for some more.

Birth mother signed sole custody relinquishments on December 20, 1963, at Norco. She was not at all ambivalent and was very cheerful. Social worker discussed with birth mother her decision, and she still felt this was the best thing she could do.

CASE SUMMARY: Birth mother was seen by the intake worker on November 1, 1963, at Norco, where she was incarcerated for narcotics. She is an 18-year-old high school graduate, pregnant and unmarried and not desiring marriage to the father of the baby. The birth mother requests adoption because she feels this would be the only plan for her to make for herself and for her child. She had plans of continuing with college. She is quite an intelligent girl, and the social worker feels that she has an excellent outlook.

The birth mother realizes the extent of her decision and does not feel that it was made without a great deal of thought. She seems to get along quite well at Norco and has a very charming personality. She and the birth father have an intellectual relationship. She does not feel that she was truly in love with him and for this reason did not want to marry him. He did not know that she was pregnant for sure.

Birth mother has made a good adjustment to the rehabilitation center and would probably be released before too long.

Social worker felt the birth mother handled her decision with maturity and will be able to reconcile her decision for herself, if later she has doubts."

Laureen, I have begun to search for your birth family. The trail, however, is 23 years old so it may take some time. I'll keep you abreast of my progress.

Yours truly,

35

/s/ Bill Will
Bill Witt
Social Service Worker V
County Adoption Service

The information in my non-identifying story provided many more pieces to the puzzle I was trying to put together. I had someone else on the job, as well. In addition to contacting the County Social Services after I returned home from England, I had also contacted the private investigator. She had begun her search, as well.

Chapter Five – Well-Adjusted

What makes us normal is knowing that we're not normal.
~Haruki Murakami

I was thrilled with all this new information. So many possibilities! I had aunts and uncles (and probably scads of cousins) and a maternal grandmother. I felt I was getting so close to finding my birth mother. The investigator I had hired was already off and running, doing what she could with her last name and little more. Now, I could provide her with all this new non-identifying information to help her with her search.

I was excited. I was also a little bit nervous. This was just the beginning, and already, I found the search to be both exhilarating and terrifying at the same time. It was difficult for me to even acknowledge all my different emotions. I also had to deal with the myriad of attitudes and opinions I encountered from other people, some not even involved with any aspect of adoption at all. Everyone had an opinion. At times during my initial search, I didn't even know how *I* was feeling. At age twenty-three and wildly ambitious, I was simply determined to forge blindly ahead and reach the finish line. I'm not sure if I would have been able to process all the emotions, even if I would have allowed myself to feel them.

I read years later about adoptees and what some adoption experts call the "adoption fog." According to psychologists and therapists who deal with adoption and adoptee issues, it refers to the hazy perception that everything about adoption is (or should be) simple, straight-forward, beautiful, and most importantly, not questioned. The reality for many adoptees is that we are told *what* to think, not taught *how* to think. We are told the perspective from which we should see our adoption. Often, we believe what we are told about being grateful, and we continue to live in a fantasy land because we are too young or too afraid to realize the truth and feel the full impact of it.

Some adoptees may stay in the fog because to feel the truth is too painful. I'm not talking about the simple truth of where you came from – I'm talking about the truth that I, and many other adoptees, face. How does being relinquished and adopted affect me and my relationships with other people? How does it hold me back? Coming out of the fog can mean enlightenment and healing, but the path is often wrought with painful realizations and personal acknowledgements.

Coming out of the fog doesn't necessarily set an adoptee on the path to search. As for me, I think when I started my search, I was still deeply entrenched in the fog. I was simply curious about family and my heritage after that crazy Varley situation with my mom and spending a year abroad. My emotions were all over the place at the time – I was just determined to move forward, headstrong, with a purpose and my right to claim my tribe. In retrospect, I wish the fog had cleared for me, at least a little, before I searched. It may have helped me to deal with what was to come.

Fog or no fog, there are so many attitudes, legalities, and different emotional reactions involved in the world of adoption. It can be overwhelming.

First, of course, there are laws, and they differ from state to state. Legally, adoption is simply a statutory process that terminates a parent's legal rights and duties toward his or her biological child and bestows similar rights and responsibilities upon the child's adoptive parents. Most states have (or had) laws mandating that the original birth records be made confidential (sealed). Confidentiality and sealed records were promoted by authorities as a way to hide the perceived negativity and the stigma associated with illegitimacy (*bastard* is a bad word!) and to advocate child welfare as the governing rule in adoption placement decisions. Sounds like good intentions, right?

Beginning in the late 1940s and continuing through the 1970s, unwed young women who found themselves pregnant faced very real and scary social, economic, and religious pressures. Many young, unmarried, pregnant women were shamed by socially conformist parents, teachers, peers, and even their own family doctors and were often sent away to live with distant relatives or to maternity homes to see out their pregnancy. These teenagers or young women were often kept in hiding until their baby was born, with the understanding that the baby would be left behind so that they could return to their former life and start over with a clean slate. The emotionally raw girls were advised to keep their secret, move on, and forget – that their best bet would be to resume life exactly where they left off before the pregnancy. As if that were possible.

Stories abound (along with documented research) about the unjust treatment of unwed mothers by social workers in maternity homes. In some cases, social workers practiced manipulating coercion tactics aimed at convincing young mothers to give up their newborn babies. The mothers-to-be were told by the authorities that they would not have the means to raise a child, even in situations where the mother came from a wealthy family or where the father of the child still wanted to be in the picture. Regardless of the actual family situation, most of the individuals and families who found themselves suddenly dealing with a pregnant, unwed, young woman were faced with the strong social mores of the time that simply rejected the idea of raising (or helping to raise) a child born out of wedlock. Many of these young mothers claim that their babies were forcibly taken from them. There was even a name given to this period of adoption: *The Baby Scoop Era* – a period that began just after World War II when unmarried mothers were shunned by society and maternity homes were in vogue. Newborn adoption rates soared as the babies were scooped up by well-meaning professional social workers and handed over to infertile couples or other families looking to create their ideal brood.

Over time, with advances in medicine and birth control, as well as socio-economic changes (like the introduction of federal funding to make family planning services more available to young and low-income individuals), rates in single mother pregnancies began to decline and so did the number of newborn adoptions. The landmark legal decision of *Roe v. Wade* in 1973, which legalized abortion in the United States, likely contributed to the decline in adoption rates due to a reduction in the number of unwanted pregnancies. Of course, this is a controversial subject. *Roe v. Wade* sparked a national debate between pro-choice and pro-life (as well as perceived moral and religious ramifications) that continues today. All these things can affect an individual's attitude about adoption. And, there is much more.

I know when I began my search more than twenty-five years ago, I thought I had educated myself as thoroughly as I could about the sociology, legalities, and psychology of adoption. I thought I was comfortable with my emotions and feelings about adoption, my adoptive family, and my birth family. I thought I knew exactly what I was feeling. Moreover, I thought I knew my rights as an individual – as an adoptee. Now, I'm not so sure I did.

Back in the 1980s, a movement had begun, headed by Florence Fisher and the Adoptees' Liberty Movement Association (ALMA), toward opening adoption records in many states (i.e., making available to adult adoptees the documents in the social services file as well as the original, unamended birth certificate). It made perfect sense to me – *of course* an adult human being is entitled to know her birth origins, ethnicity, heritage, biological roots, or whatever you want to call it. It is the true foundation for a person's basic identity. And, it would be great to have some basic medical history. It gets old writing *NOT APPLICABLE – ADOPTED* on pages and pages of medical family history forms year after year.

It would take years before the first state was successful in opening adoption records to adoptees. In November 1998, the voters of Oregon approved a ballot initiative, Measure 58, which made Oregon the first state to open, unconditionally, previously sealed records to adult adoptees. After a series of unsuccessful court challenges, the law finally went into effect on May 30, 2000. Several states followed suit, some allowing only restricted access to adoptees, some allowing court-appointed intermediaries to get involved, and still some states (like California) only allowing access upon petition to the court where the adoption was facilitated, the process determined by county procedure and based on an arbitrary finding of "good and compelling cause." As expected, some counties (and every judge within each county is different) are more lenient than others in terms of determining proof of good and compelling cause and their willingness to unseal records.

Another big draw for me and other adoptees, as simple as it sounds, was the desire to find someone who looked like me. It seemed kind of trivial when I really thought about it, given everything my adoptive family provided for me (again, *be grateful*). But, I am not alone. Every single adopted person I have ever spoken to has talked about the longing to discover where they got their blue eyes, or their thick hair, or their long legs, or their need to flail their hands wildly when they talk (yes, I wondered where I got it). It's called biological or genetic mirroring. I didn't know it had a name until just a few years ago, but it makes sense.

People who are not adopted may find it difficult to understand, but genetic mirroring is easily understood by an adopted child. In a natural biological family, a child experiences mirroring every day among members of his or her family. It's almost subliminal how it works. Similarities silently confirm belonging. Everything from physical resemblances to how a parent raises an eyebrow, walks, her tone of voice, his metabolism, athletic ability, musical talent, artistic ability, physical strength, etc. These genetic traits are fundamental to who we are, providing building blocks for a child's personality to develop and bloom naturally. This all takes place at a subconscious level and is often taken for granted by biological families.

After the birth of my first child, the genetic mirroring thing became apparent. I like to think I was starting to come out of the fog. It was so obvious that my son looked like his father's side of the family – everyone could see it. They mentioned it, too. *"He looks just like his dad!"* It was obvious to me, as well – but what hurt was that he didn't look *a thing* like me. Everyone mentioned that, too. I remember staring into his little face for hours trying to compare our noses, the shape of our eyes, chin… I got nothing. Then, as he got older, his features started to mature, and I could see hints of similarities between us, as well as similar personality traits – just like a regular biological family.

Back to adoptees and that emotional fog. Generally, adoptees are conditioned from the beginning (assuming they know they are adopted) to be grateful. After all, they were *chosen* by their adoptive parents. There is usually a story that is lovingly ingrained in the mind of an adoptee about how our biological parent or parents either were not able or did not want to take care of us. Perhaps they loved us so much, they *had* to give us away so that we would have a better life. We were saved by our adoptive parents from a life as an orphan. Adoption is a *good* thing. Without it, where would all the abandoned, unwanted children go?

The story is usually meant to be comforting. But, to a child, it can be scary. For me, as I grew older and understood a little more about what it meant to be adopted, it became clear that even though I may have been *chosen* (their word) by one family, I was *unchosen,* or rejected, by another. Of course, it's more complicated than that, but in the mind of a child, it's just that simple.

One possible effect of this way of thinking is that the adoptee can be overly focused on the needs of others. I know I was a people pleaser, always trying to please others, especially my parents in my early years. After all, the reason we were placed with adoptive parents may have been to fulfill their desire to have a child when their own biology would not allow it; to make them happy or whole.

An adopted child may also be fearful (consciously or subconsciously) of being rejected (again). Always walking on eggshells. Always trying to figure out how to fit in. This can especially manifest in the teen years and into early adulthood, with peer pressure and the struggle to be popular or to fit in with a particular group of people. I desperately needed to be wanted and accepted as a teen and throughout my twenties. My promiscuity got me the initial attention I craved, but I had difficulty maintaining relationships. Or, perhaps I put up defenses to protect myself from future losses or rejection. If it's just a one-night stand, there is no real intimacy. Or, if I dump you, you can't dump me.

There are so many theories about what an adoptee should or could feel: abandonment, gratefulness, rejection, isolation, low self-esteem, grief, and trust issues – and that's just for starters. Some psychologists or adoption experts also believe that all adoptees experience (but may not consciously acknowledge) a deep physiological and psychological trauma due to the unnatural severing of the bond between the biological mother and child at or shortly after childbirth. According to these experts, this unspeakable trauma will stay with the adoptee for the duration of his or her life, together with a deep sense of loss and grief because they are not encouraged or allowed to mourn the loss. Some experts even say that if an adoptee doesn't feel or experience that grief, he or she must simply be in denial – unable to ever break through that adoption fog. It seems then, that there can be no such thing as a well-adjusted adoptee. According to these experts, even if the adopted child seems happy or claims he is happy and content with his adoptive family, the child's actions, habits, and behaviors are really just the product of a coping strategy and compensating responses and actions to fit in where he or she does not belong. She is repressed and stunted emotionally, unable to feel the loss. Still in the fog.

The fact is, being adopted and living a normal life as an

adoptee is much more complicated than one would imagine. Even when relinquishment and adoption take place in infancy, as babies, or small children, being adopted is a lifelong *process* and part of growing up. And, each adoptee feels different.

Some adoptees will identify readily with some or all the negative feelings; others will not. Some adoptees will feel the need to search for their biological family; some will not. There isn't any one right or wrong way for an adopted individual to feel or act. Those that do choose to search will have their own reasons. I do believe, however, that any individual, adopted or not, is entitled to know his or her own identity, obtain and possess any legal or government documents that pertain to historical, genetic, and legal identification, including legal name(s), place and date of birth, and the identities of biological parents. And, don't get me started on families who don't even tell their adopted child that he or she is adopted. *Sacrilegious!*

Now you've been inside the head of an adult adoptee – sort of. But, to understand the whole picture, you also have to understand the mind of a mother who relinquishes her child to adoption. Well, good luck with that. Just like adoptees, birthmothers come in all shapes and sizes. There are birthmothers out there who believe they made the right decision in giving up their child. There are birthmothers out there who regret their decision. There are birthmothers who claim that they were coerced or shamed into relinquishing their child. And, as mentioned before, some will even claim that their babies were forcibly taken from them. Some birth mothers search for their lost children and yearn for a reunion. Some do not.

Now, you know. Or, you don't. The truth is, you know slightly more than I did when I started my search. Over the course of my journey, I've been happy, sad, frustrated, confused, angry, amazed, as well as bored, skeptical, and guarded. On occasion, my own feelings were unexpected. Sometimes, I would feel different from one hour to the next. Or, one year to the next. As I said before, it's a process and a journey. I'm still trying to find my way.

Chapter Six – You Can Lie, But You Can't Hide

We cannot live only for ourselves.
A thousand fibers connect us with our fellow men;
and among those fibers, as sympathetic threads,
our actions run as causes, and they come back to us as effects.
~Herman Melville

Our lives in this world are defined by our relationships with other people. This is not news. Connections we have with family, friends, acquaintances, and even people we don't know (yet), are what make us who we are. We are also known by the way we treat other people, our reactions to certain situations, and our capacity for empathy and compassion, or lack thereof.

Most people will say their relationships with family members are the most important bonds of all. I agree. But, what is *family*? By necessity, I define family to include not only people related to us by marriage and blood, but also those people in our lives who appreciate having us in theirs. An adoptive family falls into this category. Friends who encourage us to pursue what makes us happy, what is healthy, and what makes us feel whole are also in this category of family.

I remember my dad telling me if I paid attention, I could learn something from every single person I met in life. He was right. People (even strangers) can and will teach you life lessons

– you just need to be open. I've learned to be open to the good and the bad. I try to stay curious and open to the unknown. Fear is a factor, but I won't let the fear of the unknown or what I *think* I know about a particular situation shut me down.

I knew rejection was a possibility, but I didn't give it much thought. I didn't want to think about the prospect of my birth mother not being open to contact with me. Although I did not expect a "happily ever after" type of reunion – my birth was part of a dark time in her life, after all – I did hope that there had been enough healing in her life that she would be able to accept me. Or, at least acknowledge me. I thought she'd want to hear that I turned out okay – that the family who adopted me loved me and provided a home and environment where I was safe and where I could grow and flourish.

I waited. I had given the private investigator a copy of my non-identifying story. Even without that information, it was easy for her to positively identify my birth mother. With her last name, my date of birth, and the fact that she had given birth while serving a sentence at Frontera in California, all the investigator had to do was spend some time at the prison going through the records around the time of my birth.

Margaret Sue Michaels. Born 12 April 1945 in Chicago. Arrested August 1963. Inmate number 0738. In hospital Dec 15 thru 19th – no reason given. Arrested at the school she was attending, turned in by her step-father. Sentenced to 10 years.

Wow. Turned in by her stepfather? I remembered the details from Mr. Witt's non-identifying report. Margaret didn't remember much about her *real* father. According to the story, Margaret was very happy with her stepfather. She felt that "he was all things a father should be."

The next step was to find out what happened to Margaret after she was released from prison. The investigator hit a lot of dead ends trying to track her down. Her name was fairly common. This is where the non-identifying information proved to be so valuable. With the first names of Margaret's half-siblings and other family members, it was possible to make connections. And, these individuals were not so hard to find.

The written report I received from the private investigator chronicled her search, her contact with other family members in an attempt to locate Margaret, and finally, her initial contact with Margaret. Some of the other family members who were contacted were helpful, providing information that would lead to Margaret's whereabouts. Some of the family members were not so helpful, but not because they didn't want to help, but because they thought the investigator was on the trail of the wrong Margaret Michaels. The Margaret Michaels they all knew never had any children.

Margaret finally contacted the investigator directly, after receiving a message from a family member that the investigator was looking for her (or someone with her same name that had a child in 1963).

Report on phone call from Margaret Michaels, natural mother of Laureen Hubachek: Collect call about 10 am, very angry: "Do not tell me about my daughter, I know all that. I want to tell you how totally insensitive and unethical it was of you to contact so many people — how many have you contacted? Tell me, how many!" I told her I had only spoken to 2 individuals. One was her mother Elle. She demanded: "Don't contact anyone else! I had to do something very terrible! I had to lie to my mother!"

The investigator reminded her she had only used public information and records and that if she hadn't kept her whereabouts unlisted and hidden, she could have found her without contacting anyone else. That didn't sit well with Margaret. She lashed out at the investigator:

"Maybe that should tell you something! I didn't want to be found!"

Margaret went on to explain to the investigator that the social worker, the good and great Mr. Witt, had already contacted her. But, Mr. Witt had to seek her out through other family members, as well, just like the investigator. Mr. Witt had also contacted Elle, Margaret's mother. Elle told Mr. Witt the same thing she told the investigator: "My Margaret never had a child."

Margaret also told off the investigator – lots of colorful words were used. In the report I have, the conversation is described by the investigator as "hostile." Margaret did, however, indicate that she was considering signing the waiver of confidentiality provided to her by the social worker, and if she did decide to contact me, she would do it through Mr. Witt.

Don't get me wrong, I think it's fantastic that Mr. Witt went to the trouble to find Margaret, tell her that I was looking for her, and I had signed the waiver, *and* solicit a signed waiver from her. Honestly, if I had thought the county social services would provide me with search services for free, I would have never paid money to an investigator to do the job. And remember, there was a clause in the waiver I signed that read:

I understand that the law prohibits the Department or licensed adoption agency from soliciting, directly or indirectly the execution of such a waiver.

In fact, I had read plenty of stories about waivers simply being ignored. Unfortunately, having a Waiver of Confidentiality on file is no guarantee that a social worker or clerk won't ignore it (or be just too lazy to even look at the file to see whether there is a signed waiver in place) if a birth relative comes looking. In my family law classes, I had read about cases where an agency had had contact from both parties (adoptee and adoptive parent), but the worker or workers at the agency never let either of the parties know they were being sought. The waivers were just sitting in a file. That wasn't going to happen to me. I hired the investigator because I wanted to move forward, not just sit and wait.

The investigator called me to relay the information about the contact with my mother. I was at work at the university when she called. I was devastated that she did not want to be found. I was shattered that she did not want to know me. The conversation with the investigator left me feeling like I had been punched in the gut. My frustration overtook me after I hung up the phone. I didn't even bother to leave my desk – I laid my head on the desk and wept quietly.

How could she be so angry after all this time? It was *her* lie. Not mine. What did *I* do?

I took a step back and waited for a while. I did what I did best. I processed the situation. How could I make this situation work for me? How could I fix it? In the back of my mind, I thought, perhaps, she'd eventually make contact through Mr. Witt. She'd cool off and figure out what to tell her family, then she'd sign the waiver.

According to the investigator, who had interviewed several of Margaret's family members, Margaret had never married ("never had a man in her house") and didn't have any other children besides me, so it was just a matter of telling her mother and her siblings. I was hopeful that Margaret and I would at some point be able to meet (or at least talk on the phone) and I'd apologize.

Wait. *Apologize*? But, what did I do wrong? She was upset, that's for sure. But, if it wasn't for *her* lie, *her* twenty-two-year-old secret, *her* denial of my mere existence, we wouldn't be in this position in the first place. After twenty-two years, my near exposure of her secret might force her to deal with her own shame or whatever emotions she had suppressed over the years about giving birth and relinquishing her child for adoption. Maybe, she'd see it as an opportunity to heal. Keeping that secret for so many years must have been difficult, and maybe it was even painful. She spent her entire life hiding the truth and, more importantly, burying any emotions that may have surfaced from time to time. I had to believe she thought about me once in a while. Maybe once a year on my birthday? Anyway, this anger she was feeling now could coax her to deal with the truth and tell her family. Maybe everything would be okay… eventually.

After Margaret's initial anger wore off, surely my

biological grandmother would be happy to know about me. Maybe, I'd get to know four new aunts and uncles. Maybe, some cousins. After all, it wasn't my intention to be an intrusion or to burst into her life and claim her as my long-lost mother. I had a mother and a father and a whole family that were perfectly fine (okay, not *perfect,* but *fine*).

She *had* to want to meet me, right?

Wrong. I never heard from Mr. Witt or Margaret. I think Mr. Witt was offended that I had gotten a third-party private investigator involved. In my defense, I had no idea he was actively searching for Margaret, as well.

A few weeks after the devastating phone call from the investigator, I received the complete written report on the search in the mail, along with a short letter:

Dear Laureen,
At the request of our Director, I am enclosing your birthmother's address. The telephone is not available, but we could get it with some expense.

The investigator provided Margaret's address and confirmed through public records she was the owner of the home. Case closed.

How did I feel? I'll get the obvious out of the way: hurt and rejected, for starters. But, oddly, I also felt compassion. I really did want to apologize to Margaret. I wanted to apologize for disrupting her world. She was angry. It was my fault. I wanted to fix it. The eager-to-please adoptee.

After a week or so though, I, too, became angry. I was obviously still hurting, but I came to realize and understand that I did nothing wrong. I realized that for Margaret, there was a double whammy of shame and guilt going on back in 1963 – not only was she eighteen and pregnant, but she was serving a prison term. But, it had been over twenty-two years. Why hadn't there been any soul-searching or healing going on during that time?

Whether or not she had healed or buried her guilt and

shame, lied, was successful in her life, or whether she was living in a dumpster behind the grocery store, I knew it wasn't my fault. And, in my heart, I knew it wasn't her fault, either. She was well into her "do-over," as promised to her by the system. Enter me, like an unexpected and unwelcomed house guest.

Either way, I still believed I had a right to information. Information about my birth, my ancestry, my heritage, other family, and even my birthfather. And, what about medical information? I needed to know my story.

Chapter Seven – A Fabulous Life

Recovery can take place only within the context of relationships;
it cannot occur in isolation.
~Judith Lewis Herman

I have read stories of adoptees just showing up at a birth family member's home: *Surprise! I'm your long-lost daughter!* Hugs all around… happily ever after… blah, blah, blah… I could never do that.

Yet, I had Margaret's address. It was only a thirty-minute drive from my front door to hers. All this time… so close, and yet, so far.

I wondered if we had we ever inadvertently crossed paths. Had I ever seen her in a crowd, or maybe up close and not even known it? It was possible. Not likely, however. During the years I was a child and teenager, she had no reason to be hanging around anywhere I would be. She didn't have any other kids.

I mapped out the directions and wrote them down, using the good ol' *Thomas Guide*, but I never made the trip. I was scared. I figured I should already know what to expect. She could have reached out to me, but she didn't. She could have sent a message through Mr. Witt, but she didn't. Perhaps, she was scared, too.

I also knew from the information I received from Mr. Witt and the investigator that Margaret had never gotten married and she had never had any other children. What was she afraid of? She wasn't keeping secrets from her "kept" children or a husband. Why was she so angry?

Yes, there was sadness and anger on my part, but it didn't take much time for those feelings to pass, or at least diminish. I'm a strong person and a pretty good judge of character. I can usually process other people's actions and emotions, as well as my own, and figure out how to fit in and move forward. I've lived most of my life that way: watching and listening to people and trying to figure out how to fit into *their* world. Adoptees tend to be good at that.

I processed the situation at hand. My conclusion: Margaret was initially angry because I had nearly upset her entire world (whatever that world *was*). I had almost exposed her secret. Of course, that was devastating to her. She lashed out in anger. But, here was *my* problem: her world was built around a lie. I was an adult person that exists in this world. She was basically denying my existence.

On the one hand, I wanted to respect her privacy. On the other hand, I wanted answers. And, what of *privacy?* I was struggling to figure out how that word even fit in this situation. Was she obligated to give me the information? Legally, no.

But, we're all human beings. We all have the same basic needs and wants, beginning with our identity. At the very least, I believed a moral obligation existed: a woman who chooses adoption for her child should take full responsibility for that decision. That decision changes the identity of another human being. I didn't need a relationship or even ongoing contact – what I needed was meaningful communication and information. Then, we could be done, if that was the way she wanted it.

I decided to write a letter to Margaret in 1987, about six months after I had found her. I don't remember exactly what I wrote. I know I did my best to explain my disappointment. I also defended my actions in seeking her out. I told her I was "okay," and I just wanted to ask some questions.

Margaret responded. Her letter was handwritten on letterhead from The Omni Hotel in South Carolina. She was traveling for work. She got right down to business.

Laureen,

I was surprised to receive your letter – and disappointed. You need to understand that I strongly feel it was wrong for any records to be opened to you. To me, it's more than an invasion of privacy. I actually feel that by such a disclosure on the part of authorities I trusted, I have been betrayed and violated!

I can't believe that any good can come from any further contact, and I don't want to meet or talk, nor to continue a correspondence. But since you are interested, I will take the time to comment on a couple of things.

Margaret went on to tell me about herself – how she was "strong" and "self-sufficient" and could never be influenced by others. She had no regrets in life and had lived her life exactly the way she wanted.

Never have I ever done anything that I either felt to be wrong, or later regretted. As a result, I am well-pleased with my life. I have a good education and the kind of job most people can only dream of. So, you see, I have never wondered about you, nor did I expect that you would wonder about me. I hope that I have now told you enough that you can comfortably let go of your desire for further contact.

I had reached out for a connection, but now I felt even more detached than ever.

It seemed to me that Margaret was defending her actions in life (one of which was giving me up for adoption) and telling me how wonderful her life had been because of it. She didn't need me. She didn't need to even know about me.

The closing of her letter hurt the most. Maybe, I was reading too much into it.

Got to run. I've got a plane to catch.

Margaret

P.S. Sorry to have left your last name off the address on the envelope, but I tossed your envelope before realizing that your last name was not on the letter.

I felt so small. So insignificant. Maybe I should feel lucky? At least she was able to scratch out a letter to me in between traveling the world for her totally fabulous and fantastic job.

The information she provided about herself was guarded, and it seemed she was trying to intimidate me. She succeeded. She didn't need me in her life. She was educated, successful, quite pleased with herself, and... well, quite pleased with herself.

I didn't write back... right away.

Chapter Eight – Quiet, But Too Well-Poised

The narcissist is governed by his or her feelings,
the decent person is governed by his or her obligations.
~Dennis Prager

I understand the secrecy. I understand the shame. But, hopefully, with time comes understanding and healing. We process; we evolve. And come on, what about common decency? When a woman keeps a secret such as giving birth and giving away a baby, the continuation of the lies and the shame associated with that secret should not follow her *or her child* for *life*.

I'd like to clear up the matters of secrecy and betrayal once and for all. More importantly, I'd like to clear up the issue of privacy. A birth mother may have been told that the birth records are legally sealed, but, in reality, privacy could not have been and was not promised or guaranteed. How can this sort of privacy even be expected? We're talking about another human being's identity and existence in this world.

Putting emotions aside, in fact, privacy and anonymity are *not* (and never have been) promised to a birth mother. The true intent of sealing the original birth certificate (and concocting a new one) was never meant to protect the birthparents. The two primary reasons for sealing original birth records back when the practice began (depending on the state, likely sometime before 1940) were: 1) to keep birthparents from interfering with adoptive families, and 2) to protect adopted children from the stigma of illegitimacy. Birthparents were never guaranteed anonymity under any state law or in any adoption/relinquishment documents they may have signed.

In my heart, I knew I hadn't done anything wrong, unlawful, illegal, prohibited, criminal, or even irregular. So, why did I feel so bad? *Guilty*, even? I knew there were many adoptees before me who dove into the unknown with their desire to search for their biological family. It's normal. It's even expected. All adoptees wonder about their origins. I was one of those who took action.

Even for individuals who were raised with their biological families, questions about relatives (What's up with our crazy uncle?), ancestors (maybe you're related to Annie Oakley, or you share a common ancestor with Frank Sinatra), and family history abound. Genealogy and building family trees are more than just hobbies. Genealogy is big business.

As for birthparents, studies have indicated the overwhelming majority are not opposed to being found by their adult children. Some even seek out their children after years of longing and regret. Not Margaret. But seriously, she was not even curious about me?

Always the optimist, I simply pushed any thoughts of a second rejection aside. I knew from research, as well as from all the happy reunions were all over the television (true stories and made-for-television dramas, alike), that the likelihood of a birth mother rejecting contact from an adult child was extremely small.

Margaret was one of the one to five percent who didn't want to be found. But, *why*? How can facing the truth be that terrible? I started out by just trying to rationalize that she may just be the sort of person I wouldn't want to know anyway. It didn't have anything to do with adoption. Besides, I knew plenty of people who grew up with their biological families and were trying to create serious distance from parents, siblings, or other family members for some reason or another. Don't we all know someone who hasn't spoken to his or her mother or father or a sibling for months or even years? Hurt feelings, stubbornness, money issues… whatever the reason, I never understood such extreme reactions and emotions. When I thought about Margaret's rejection of me, I tried to chalk it up to not understanding people. I must admit, in the back of my mind, I thought (or hoped) maybe she needed time to get acquainted with the idea of my presence in her world.

But, the lie continued. I moved on. I graduated from college, got a great job, started my paralegal career, and began paying off student loans. Life became more stable, routine. With that, the promiscuity thing got boring and I wanted to try making my own family. It didn't take long for me to meet a decent guy, fall in love, and get married. After a year of marriage, I was pregnant. I was proud of myself, too. I did it all in the right order. Like it mattered.

I was twenty-seven when Zachary was born in 1991. Aside from his dark-brown eyes and dark-brown hair, both of which his father also had, we had *no* similar features I could readily identify. The question often asked was, *"Does he look like anyone on your side of the family?"*

At this point in my life, my adoption story became more like an elaborate comedy routine. If my adoption or adoption in general ever came up in conversation for any reason, I would laugh it off and almost always make a joke of it. It was a punch line. I could easily one-up anyone's tragic family story, whether it be about adoption or something else.

What? Your dad left your mom and your twelve brothers and sisters when you were just five years old? Big deal! I was born in prison! Yeah, a prison baby! Imagine that! One month premature, too – born to a drug-addicted, beatnik hippie, convict mother! That explains a lot, right? Given up for adoption… [snort, snort]… and then, guess what? I found her just a few years ago – and I was rejected *again*!

Laughter all around. Hilarious.

Rejected *again*. So, why would I go back for more?

The feeling of being adopted (and twice rejected) had

morphed in my brain into this imaginary, unpredictable fairy who followed me around. She was always there, lurking. Sometimes she was quiet, sometimes she was crazy, taunting me, pushing me to do something, *anything*! Just go knock on Margaret's door unannounced. Or, call her mother, Elle. That would get Margaret's attention. The mercurial fairy had wild ideas sometimes. Other times, she just wanted me to forget about it and move on.

The more I thought about it, the more I could not accept that Margaret didn't want to know me. I could not accept that she could not (or would not) acknowledge my existence and my value. I read and re-read her letter – it was all about Margaret – clearly, she felt like she needed to defend herself (and her decision to relinquish me) and do her best to let me know it was "the right thing to do." Not only was it the right thing to do, but her life was fantastic because of it. Super fantastic and full of travel and exotic stuff and a dream job and no time to remember my name. So super wonderful that she doesn't even think about me. And, she doesn't want to meet me or even communicate with me.

Truth be told, it was Zachary who made me think about it all again. Did he look like my family? And surely, Margaret would want to know about a grandson. Her only child (me) had given her a grandchild.

Oh, yuck. Just thinking like that felt weird. I didn't give her anything. Zachary was *mine*. Not hers. But, there was something that made me want to give her one more chance. And, I still believed I was entitled to know about my origins, my history, my ancestry, and medical and health information. I had to make contact again. The fairy was egging me on.

I wrote another letter. I tried to be more careful with my words. I already knew she'd be resistant to any kind of contact or any kind of exchange of information – she said so in her first letter. I sent a picture of me holding Zach. I think he was about eight months old. This was 1992. My hair was still big.

Even though I was careful with my words, I couldn't help disclosing my bold thoughts about her secret. I may have suggested to her that she might be insecure – not able to deal with her past in a manner that would allow her to recognize other people's feelings. Her secret (or lie, depending on how you want to spin it) was about something that happened over twenty-five years ago. It could not make me disappear. I told her about Zach – I told her I wondered where he got his nose and other features.

I knew Margaret didn't want a relationship. I didn't need one, and I told her so. I understand every human being has the right to decline a relationship with another individual. A birth mother should have the right to say "no thank you" to her birth daughter's request for a meeting or an ongoing relationship. Likewise, an adoptee has the right to decline a request from a birth parent. It's no different for biological families – relatives are "cut off" all the time. Well, it's a little different because most biological families, for the most part, already have a solid identity base and knowledge of family history – family history is usually what causes the rift in the first place. In any event, relationships between friends and even family members (biological or not) cannot be legislated. I understood that.

Please, just answer the questions, Margaret. Meaningful communication is all I ask for. The more honest and open you can be (I'll be patient), the sooner I will feel comfortable leaving you alone.

A second letter from Margaret arrived. Her tone was somewhat softer and less agitated, but her message was the same. Her opening paragraph tore the scab right off the wound.

Dear Laureen,

Each contact from you (or contact from others on your behalf) has so far been such a negative experience that I was made to feel that no good could come from further contact.

What? She was *made to feel* that further contact would be bad? I didn't understand. It was my fault? About her "lie," as I called it:

> *I find no conflict between the fact that I value my privacy and the fact that I very much like who I am. One thing that I especially like about me is the fact that I had the common sense at a very early age to make the difficult decision to put a child up for adoption. And I hope that you can accept that valuing privacy is not synonymous with being insecure!*

Well, Margaret, I especially like that about you, too.

I found it a little weird that she referred to her "common sense" and the fact that she made a "difficult decision to put a child up for adoption" (*hello* – I'm right here!). *Choice?* Did she even have a choice?

Unwed mothers in the 1950s and 1960s who were not even in prison have spoken and written about how they felt they didn't have a choice about keeping a child. They were coerced by authorities or made to believe there were no other options. Margaret's situation was a little different, however. Margaret was in state prison in 1963 (there were no prison nurseries back then), and she *believed* she actually made a *thoughtful choice?* If she had not been in prison, I wonder what her choice would have been. Would I even be here today?

Margaret went on to admonish me about what I *needed to accept* (accidents happen sometimes) and what I *needed to understand* (what it was like to be pregnant and unmarried in the 1960s). How her decision in the middle of this *bad situation* was *exactly the correct action under the circumstances.*

Margaret – please hear me now: *Of course,* you made the right decision to put your daughter up for adoption. No one is arguing you did something wrong in that regard. No one is asking you to think about that decision at this point. I don't want to think about it (what if abortion had been an available choice?).

The reality is that not only did Margaret's *decision* "salvage" her life (her word choice), but it obviously salvaged mine, too!

Margaret rehashed the whole private investigator incident (callous and without a "shred of human decency"), as well as the communication with the wonderful Mr. Witt ("a man who worked for the county who violated the court order"). Basically, she was still trying to get me to believe that everyone was against her and out to harm her, or disrupt her wonderful lie… I mean, life.

She did attempt to address my question about Zach's features. She wrote about her nose:

> *My nose is my most distinctive feature, and I'm not fond of it! I've enclosed 2 pictures of me so you can see if in fact that is where your son got his nose. There [sic] not very good pictures, but you see, I always try to pose for pictures in a manner that does not show my nose very well, with the result that I had to search extensively to find any that shows it at all, and these were the best angles I could come up with.*

Dark hair and dark eyes. Zach didn't have her nose. Neither did I. Finally, one last hurrah for how fabulous her life was:

> *Now I have to ask you a favor. If you really feel you ever have to contact me again, please write to me at work instead of at home. If you mark the envelope "Personal & Confidential," no one will open it. I've enclosed a card so you will have the address. I've been there for 22 years, so you're more likely to find me there in the future than in the same home address.*

I wasn't expecting hearts and flowers. But, maybe a question or two (or, God forbid, a compliment) about Zach. How about asking me how I had been? How was I doing? How did I feel? What did I want to know?

I never wrote to her again.

PART II: JONATHAN

Chapter Nine – Still Untold

Anyone who isn't confused really doesn't understand the situation.
~Edward R. Murrow

I had my fiftieth birthday in 2013. No one asked me if I was having a mid-life crisis. I must have been holding it together. Or, maybe it was just so obvious that no one wanted to ask. *Don't look her in the eye – she'll crack, for sure!*

I'd call it a mid-life *identity* crisis. It had been over twenty years since the second letter from Margaret. I'll just go ahead and say the word I keep avoiding: *Rejection.* It's a word that is commonly used in the adoption community, but at this point, I was reluctant to label her treatment of me as rejection. She didn't reject me, she rejected the *idea* of me. She didn't even know me. How could she reject me?

To be relinquished at birth for adoption is one thing. That's Margaret rejecting the idea of being a mother. She was young and unprepared (not to mention a little preoccupied with serving a prison sentence), and a baby did not fit with her plans. Adoption was her salvation (and mine).

But, to be rejected later in life by the woman who gave birth to me – to be rejected as a grown, rational adult (for all intents and purposes) asking questions about the very core of my being, seeking answers that most people take for granted – is something completely and utterly different. I read an article some time ago written by another adoptee who described the feeling of rejection by adoptees quite simply, but completely.

I'm paraphrasing, but the gist of it went like this:

Me: I exist.

Margaret: I wish you didn't.

Exactly.

I cannot control how Margaret feels. I can only control my reaction. And, I'll admit it hurt, but I'm not the type to kick something around forever. It happened once (well, maybe twice… or three times), but my life is full of other moments. Pretty darn good moments. Why wallow in the negative? I forged ahead, with my head still in the fog.

By this time, my son, Zach, was twenty-three years old. He was out on his own, happily finding his way with his music. Quite a bit of other stuff had happened in the span of those twenty-three years. By stuff, I mean life: divorce, a second marriage, and another son.

It might be worth noting that my first marriage ended just shortly after Zachary was born. While I was pregnant with Zach, I discovered his father was having an affair with a nineteen-year-old girl he had hired to work in his office. That ruined everything. I was a failure at creating that perfect (or at least normal) family. But, regardless of who hurt whom, I wasn't going to let *him* control the situation and be the one to leave me and Zach. No way was I going to be abandoned again. We stayed together and tried to make it work until after Zach was born, and then I secretly planned my escape from the marriage. I filed for divorce and left him when Zach was just eight months old.

I got married again in 1997. Garrett (son number two) was born in the year 2000. When he was small, everyone said he was the spitting image of his dad. Here we go again. Garrett still looks like his dad today. Light hair, blue eyes, fair skin. Once again, I was gazing into the face of my child looking for similarities and any sign of familiarity. *Nothing.*

Over the years, I didn't think too much about Margaret or my biological origins. I was too busy with living in the present. For heaven's sake, I was a career-minded single mom for a while. That's complicated. And then, during my second marriage, things got even more confusing.

In addition to my paralegal career, my boys were growing, and they were keeping me busy with their school activities and sports. Then, in 2003, both of my adoptive parents died. My dad died of pancreatic cancer. It was quick and painful and just plain awful. My mother died forty-five days later of an apparent heart attack.

By the time my dad became ill with cancer, my mom was already struggling with emphysema, attached to an oxygen machine twenty-four hours a day, and requiring constant care. My dad was caring for her until he got sick. Once he was in the hospital, I did my best, traveling between the hospital to check on my dad and back to my childhood home in another city to check on mom, cook and clean, and make sure she was stocked up with her generic vodka and cigarettes. She was still smoking and swigging the swill until the very end.

I was talking to my dad in the hospital one day about not wanting to buy anymore vodka or cigarettes for mom. It was killing her, and I hated doing it. From his deathbed, my dad said, "Go ahead and get her the vodka and cigarettes. I'm worried about the old girl." So, I bought the deadly items for her on my weekly shopping trips. Dad was right. At that point, what difference would it make anyway? It made me crazy knowing she was removing her oxygen supply several times a day so she could have a few pulls of her nicotine fix. She was aware of the danger, but with dad gone, the thought of losing her friend in cigarettes was more daunting than the prospect of dying.

You know what else happened over the course of those years? Science and technology. On the technology side, computers were everywhere, connecting everything and everyone. The World Wide Web grew and evolved, with its databases, easy access to public information, instant communication, and sharing of personal data via social media.

On the science side, I was especially fascinated with the advancements in DNA testing. My husband, Guy, is a former prosecutor who worked for years with people who do forensic DNA testing for criminal cases. DNA testing had evolved to allow cold cases to be solved in an instant. It was fascinating, but I wasn't as interested in crime solving as I was interested in the way DNA testing was being used for health and genealogy research. Talk about an evolution.

One company, *23andMe*, claimed DNA genetic testing may be able to predict risk for certain diseases and medical conditions. This would be helpful for adoptees, who, for the most part, have no information about their family medical history. In addition, DNA testing was being used to reveal information about family backgrounds and familial traits, ethnic heritage, and ancestral history. And finally, the newer autosomal DNA testing could accurately identify relationships between family members by comparing DNA segments. Put technology (easy access via the Internet) and DNA testing together, and you've got a huge triumph not just for adoptees, but for anyone interested in researching their family tree. The bigger the database to compare your genetic results (thank you, World Wide Web), the more useful and meaningful results you'll get. Genius.

It would be a relief to finally be able to shed some light on any potential future health concerns or possible predisposition to certain illnesses. I sure wasn't going to get that information from relatives. My boys were entitled to this information, as well.

Luckily, as science and technology evolved, prices for the commercial DNA genetic testing became more affordable. What cost nearly $500 in 2009 came down in price to around $99 by late 2012. I decided to use the autosomal DNA testing service offered by the company *23andMe*. In 2013, I spit into a test tube and sent it in. And then, things got weird.

Chapter Ten – Hope Springs Eternal

Hope itself is a species of happiness, and, perhaps,
the chief happiness which this world affords;
but, like all other pleasures immoderately enjoyed,
the excesses of hope must be expiated by pain.
~Samuel Johnson

I had embraced the science – DNA genetic research and testing as a tool to reveal or predict health risks. Everybody was doing it. I jumped on the bandwagon. And, I waited.

I had also embraced the technological side of things. The World Wide Web was my friend. My silent partner in my adoption journey. My lifeline, if you will.

I was sure Margaret was relieved not to have heard from me for more than two decades, and I wasn't about to try to reach out to her again, but I was still curious, and I still had questions. At age fifty, that damn fairy had started hovering again. What about my birth father? Who was he? Did he know about me? I was fairly certain Margaret was the only person who knew his identity. I also knew Margaret wasn't going to give up that information. Margaret had no other children, but what if I had siblings on my father's side? And, what about Margaret's siblings – my aunts and uncles – some of whom were closer to my age than Margaret's? Did they know about me?

Thanks to the Internet – that wondrous gem of technology – I was able to keep track of Margaret's whereabouts over the years. Not in a crazy stalker kind of way, but more like a let's-see-what-she's-up-to once a year kind of way. I was keeping hope alive.

The Internet also made it easy to find Margaret's siblings. She had four half-siblings – I knew this from the non-identifying information I received years ago. Over the two decades since I had received the non-identifying puzzle pieces, I had been able to roughly put some of the pieces together. Early on, it was difficult. The names of Margaret's siblings were fairly common. But, then Facebook came along, making it easier to find them, knowing generally where they all lived (or had lived at one time or another). Luckily, three of Margaret's four siblings were active on Facebook. I eventually found them, but was initially terrified to reach out to them. I knew how Margaret felt, and that scared me. I wondered how they felt, or if they even knew about me. How much did they know? How close were they to Margaret? How would they react if I did reach out? And, if they didn't know about me, would they even believe such a story?

As I waited for the health results from *23andMe*, the fairy and I crafted a way to reach out to Margaret's siblings. I'll admit, it was a bit underhanded, but I thought it was genius. It was also a rogue attempt to reach out via the World Wide Web to see if anyone could help me find my birth father. A sort of *focused* rogue attempt.

I got the idea from the Internet, of course. Over the last few years, there had been a growing trend of people using social media and the magic of sharing to find other people. People were personally advertising for all sorts of reasons: missed connections, missing persons, locating people after natural disasters or even after terror attacks. What I found most interesting, of course, was the growing number of adoptees and birth parents searching by posting pictures, information and pleas for assistance online that pulled desperately on heartstrings. The power and reach of social media were undeniable. Like a cheesy 1980s shampoo commercial… *I told two friends, and they told two friends, and so on, and so on…* (I'm really dating myself with that one).

Margaret was not on *Facebook*, but with the mention of her name and circumstances of her pregnancy and my birth in prison right out there on *Facebook*, it would no doubt ring a bell with one of the siblings. Someone would have to connect. Maybe the siblings had information. Maybe they knew things about Margaret and my birth father. Maybe the door would finally be opened so that Margaret and I could connect on some level. I had no delusions about a relationship, but I still had hope for answers.

I prepared my social media plea, which included some photos of me as a baby and from my childhood, along with a current photo, and a simple request for help in finding my birthfather. I disclosed my date of birth, location of birth (California Institute for Women, Frontera, in Chino), my birthmother's name (that would get the attention of Margaret's siblings) and some other incidentals that would leave no doubt in the siblings' minds that I was legit.

I posted it on my Facebook timeline in July 2013. Here's the underhanded part: I simultaneously sent friend requests to Margaret's three siblings that were on Facebook. That way, they were sure to see my post.

It worked. The three siblings accepted my friend requests. One of Margaret's sisters reached out to me right away via private message. We made introductions on Facebook and started a cautious conversation via email. Joannie confirmed that none of Margaret's siblings knew anything about her being pregnant and giving birth while she was in prison. Joannie also told me she spoke to Margaret on the phone shortly after her discovery of me via Facebook to discuss the news of this *new* family member. Margaret was indignant; she didn't deny that I was her child, but she made it clear to Joannie that she was still not open to contact and really had no interest in discussing the situation (past or present) with any of her siblings (or me). I wasn't surprised. But, I was still hopeful.

Chapter Eleven – Who's Your Daddy?

Learn from yesterday, live for today, hope for tomorrow.
The important thing is not to stop questioning.
~Albert Einstein

Thank you, science and technology. *23andMe* gave me a genetically clean bill of health. The health information provided to me by *23andMe* included whether I was at risk for certain diseases, whether I had carrier status for some diseases, my propensity for adverse drug response to certain medications, genetic traits and information regarding other health labs established by *23andMe*. *23andMe* detected a couple of genes that indicated an elevated risk for a few non-life-threatening conditions (psoriasis and restless leg syndrome, for example), but nothing for me to worry about. As for the possibility of any serious, inherited conditions, my test results detected no mutations or gene variants that might indicate any of the ones screened for by *23andMe*. I was lucky – I received my health results before *23andMe* suspended their health-related genetic testing to comply with the U.S. Food and Drug Administration's directive in December of 2013.

After I received the health results, I played around with the ancestry section of the site. I was fascinated to find out my heritage included German, British, and Irish. Given my dark hair and eyes and my propensity for arguing, raising my voice in exciting situations, and talking with my hands (flailing uncontrollably, actually), I figured there would be a bit of Italian in me. But, no. Nevertheless, I was enchanted with being British and Irish. Turns out I was visiting *my* ancestors' homeland when I spent that year abroad in college. My adoptive mother would have loved to have known that. And, with the Irish bit, I secretly imagined that I was related to Bono. My past, including my heritage and ancestry, had always been something I could play with in my imagination. Adoptees do that a lot.

I don't know why I didn't explore the *DNA Relatives* section of *23andMe*. I already knew who my biological mother was. I also knew she didn't have any other children. What were the odds I'd find anything or anyone meaningful through a DNA match? First, I didn't imagine my birth father was looking for me. Most likely, he was not even aware of my existence. And, given his age (early 70s), I didn't think he'd be spitting into a plastic tube and getting in touch with his genes just for the fun of it. So, I didn't venture to the *DNA Relatives* section of the website for weeks.

Then, a few weeks after analyzing the health and ancestry data, I received an email from *23andMe*. It was a conduit email, from a potential relative.

Hi,

Through our shared DNA, 23andMe has identified us as relatives. Our predicted relationship is 4th Cousin, with a likely range of 3rd to 6th Cousin. Would you like to explore our relationship?

Fourth (maybe even sixth) cousin? *Whoop de doo.* Because I had no blood relatives I actually *knew*, except for my own boys, the possibility of identifying a fourth cousin did not rouse any sort of curiosity in me. Even if he was related to me on my paternal side, how would I know? An individual who was a potential DNA match on *23andMe* would probably inquire about lineage by requesting a list of known surnames. A common surname could help someone putting together a family tree to fill in the blanks. I was afraid my blanks went much deeper than that. I didn't think I could help anyone with the information I had. And, I didn't have a list of surnames. It just didn't occur to me how this distant match might help me.

I ignored that first message. But, then I got a few more. They were all distant relations and seemed so obscure to me… third to sixth cousin, fourth to distant cousin, etc. I finally went online at *23andMe* to check out the DNA Relatives section. I knew I could shut off the notifications if I wanted to, but I must admit, I was a little curious to see what kind of matches I had and how *23andMe* presented the information.

Just as I expected, it was a little weird… and a lot overwhelming. The summary, with a link to the details revealing potential relatives looked like this:

Close Family	1st Cousins	2nd & 3rd Cousins	4th Cousins	Distant Cousins
1	0	0	232	762

DNA RELATIVES

762 potential relatives? This was just a few weeks after getting my results, and I had over 750 matches? Sheesh! What does one even do with this kind of information? Distant cousins? I was overcome by the same feeling I had when I found those scads of Varleys for my mother in England over thirty years ago.

I thought about it a while. Maybe I *should* care about distant cousins. I knew making contact with these distant relatives was one way to find common ancestors and build a family tree. But, how would I start? I didn't have a family tree. Or, even a shrub. Or, a weed.

Then, I saw it. *"1 CLOSE FAMILY."* What? Who? I

clicked on the link, but before *23andMe* would reveal any details, a warning popped up. I had to confirm I *really, really* wanted the information. This was not a game.

23andMe asked for two layers of consent before it would reveal my close family relationship. First, I was given the opportunity to turn off the "relative finder" function, which shows relations as close as second cousins. After opting in, if *23andMe* has found any close relatives (closer than a second cousin), a warning is presented via popup that explains how this evidence of a close family relationship might be unexpected and even upsetting in some cases. *Upsetting?* Been there. Done that (with Margaret). Of course, I wanted to know.

You may learn information about yourself that you do not anticipate. Such information may provoke strong emotion.

Thanks, *23andMe*. I was scared. But, I clicked "proceed" anyway.

Male

Predicted Relationship

Father

50% DNA shared, 23 segments

Father?! What the *hell?* My *biological father?!* *23andMe* found my biological father when no one else (except for probably Margaret) knew who he was? Boy, howdy, this was *not* a game. Or, was it? I felt like I had won the lottery! I just needed someone to confirm the winning ticket.

Still, I wasn't sure what the data meant:

50.0% shared, 23 segments

But, I sure as hell knew what *Father* meant. I would do the science and technical research later. I had to contact this guy.

Initial contact had to be made through *23andMe*. I could hardly think straight as I typed out a message to *Father*. On August 6, 2013, I wrote:

> *Hi,*
>
> *I am contacting you because 23andMe has identified you as a relative of mine because of our shared DNA. 23andMe has predicted, through our DNA match, that you are my biological father. You won't recognize my name, because I was adopted and bear the name of my adoptive parents. However, my birth mother's name is Margaret Michaels. I hope that the name Margaret Michaels is familiar to you, although it was 50 years ago and I understand that it was a difficult time for both of you. I hope that you will respond to my message and that you are interested in exploring our relationship. I look forward to hearing from you!*
>
> *Laureen Pittman (original birth certificate reads: "Baby Girl Michaels")*

Crazy, right? But, it can happen. *23andMe* even said so. I frantically searched the website for some sort of confirmation of the match, something that would allow me to accept the accuracy of information.

> *You can be confident that the matches listed in DNA Relatives are your relatives, even though they may be quite distantly related to you. The vast majority of relatives found by DNA Relatives share a common ancestor within the last five to ten generations. A few may be more distantly related. There is, however, the possibility of finding a much closer relative – including a parent or sibling. (23andMe Customer Care: What Can 23andMe Do For Me If I Am Adopted?)*

I started searching the Internet for stories of adoption DNA matches. Turns out it had happened before. The stories I read amazed me. Some scared me. Some were happy endings; some were new beginnings. Sometimes the results were, indeed, unexpected. This was the headline of one article I came across: *Whoops. How DNA Site 23andMe Outed Parents Who Gave Their Baby Up For Adoption.* And, how about this blog post title: *When Family Ties Turn Into Knots.* Of course, I was attracted to the stories that tore through the carefully crafted lies, revealing life-changing information and enlightenment to people seeking the truth. Like me.

Science and technology have this incredible way of uncovering secrets. I waited for my secrets to be revealed.

Chapter Twelve – DNA Doesn't Lie

The good thing about science is that it's true
whether or not you believe in it.
~Neil deGrasse Tyson

W hat did it mean?
50.0% shared, 23 segments

23andMe tests autosomal DNA. To break it down as simply as possible (I'm no scientist and most of what I've read about DNA and genetics goes right over my head, so it helps me to keep it simple), there are three different types of DNA tests that are applicable for family history purposes. Y-chromosome DNA tests explore the direct paternal line and are typically interpreted within the context of a surname study. Mitochondrial DNA tests can be used for genealogical matching purposes on the direct maternal line. Autosomal DNA tests can be used to find genetic matches with close relatives, and more distant cousins, on all the different lines (through both males and females).

Human cells have twenty-three pairs of chromosomes: twenty-two pairs of autosomes and one pair of sex chromosomes, called allosomes. Certain genetic traits are linked to a person's sex and are passed on through the sex chromosomes. The autosomes contain the rest of the genetic hereditary information.

LAUREEN PITTMAN

The examination of autosomal DNA has become highly useful in the study of genetic genealogy. I'm oversimplifying here, but basically, when comparing your autosomal DNA with another person, if you share identical *segments* of DNA, you share a recent common ancestor. A segment of DNA is technically called a *nucleotide* and, in layman's terms, is just a building block of DNA. The length and number of these identical segments will predict how close (or recent) the relationship is. The more autosomal DNA that you have in common with another person, the more closely related you are.

A child receives 47-50% of his autosomal DNA from each of his parents, and similarly on average a child receives about 25% of his autosomal DNA from each of his four grandparents. The chromosomes recombine, or mix, as they are passed down from parent to child, so the size of possible shared segments gets successively smaller with each generation, as illustrated by the chart below.

50%	Mother, father, siblings
25%	Grandfathers, grandmothers, aunts, uncles, half-siblings, double first cousins
12.5%	Great-grandparents, first cousins, great-uncles, great-aunts, half-aunts/uncles, half-nephews/nieces
6.25%	First cousins once removed, half first cousins
3.125%	Second cousins, first cousins twice removed
1.563%	Second cousins once removed
0.781%	Third cousins, second cousins twice removed
0.391%	Third cousins once removed
0.195%	Fourth cousins
0.0977%	Fourth cousins once removed
0.0488%	Fifth cousins
0.0244	Fifth cousins once removed
0.0122%	Sixth cousins
0.0061%	Sixth cousins once removed
0.00305%	Seventh cousins

| 0.001525% | Seventh cousins once removed |
| 0.000763% | Eighth cousins |

(Data from International Society of Genetic Genealogy)

I spent an entire weekend on the Internet researching and trying to figure out what *50%, 23 segments* meant. Based on what I found (and was able to understand), I was convinced that the *Father* that *23andMe* had matched me with was indeed my biological father. But, would he be convinced?

I was emotional. A little scared. Afraid of what might happen next. Or, maybe I was afraid that nothing would happen next.

Sometimes, I just go full steam ahead. Everything makes sense and things happen. Not always good things. Even when good things do happen in this crazy search, it can be scary. I had enough raw data and information (names, addresses, phone numbers, etc.) to power through and get the answers I thought I needed. But, what if I upset people? Maybe, I didn't need the answers. Or, maybe if I just kept telling myself I didn't need the answers, I could move forward and get the answers and not be affected by the consequences.

Frankly, I was emotionally exhausted at this point. I don't know why I got a bug up my ass in 2013 to reignite my search. Because I turned fifty? Maybe. Emotionally, it was an all-consuming project. It was getting difficult to accomplish stuff on my normal day-to-day to-do list. One day, I would be motivated by my progress and new connections, and the next, I would be frustrated by a mere stranger's reaction and attitude and the emotional doors being slammed in my face.

I knew, however, that I was fully attached to the outcome of this whole thing. Plus, that damn fairy was still nagging me.

I didn't hear back right from this guy *23andMe* was calling my *Father*, so I had some time to process things. *Just step back and wait*, I told myself. Wait for a sign or a connection.

And then, *BAM!* I finally heard from my biological father. It seemed like an eternity, but he actually responded within a few days of receiving my message via *23andMe*.

Jonathan Winter, *Father*, wrote:

What is very strange about this is that I am from the same town as Margaret and although not exactly 50 years ago, the love of my life was named Marian Michaels. We met in school. I was 16 and she was 14. To make a long story short we were together for 8 years at which time the relationship broke up because of my drug use. Because I loved her so much, I went away and straightened myself out.

Unfortunately, I had destroyed the trust between us and we went our separate ways. I eventually married and had a daughter and Marian married and had a son and a daughter. Years later, my wife passed away due to cancer. Marian's husband had died one year earlier.

Today Marian and I are best of friends and often visit one another.

Laureen, your inquiry has piqued my interest. There are so many coincidences in our stories. I would enjoy getting to know you.

My very best to you,
Jonathan Winter

That was odd. My bio mom was *Margaret* Michaels. His first love's name was *Marian* Michaels. The same age. In the same town. Was this some other weird piece of an even more twisted puzzle? It didn't make sense. I wrote back to Jonathan and gave him more details. I summarized all the information from the non-identifying data I had received from the wonderful Mr. Witt (I eventually gave him a copy of the non-identifying paperwork with *all* of the details). Now, he would know that I *knew* he had been arrested with Margaret. It also gave him a bit of backstory about his relationship with Margaret. That would jog his memory. His story about "going away to straighten himself out" made sense to me – that had to be the time he served in prison. *Had to be…* right? And, what about the DNA? I knew Margaret was my bio mom. Not someone named Marian. And, the DNA was solid confirmation (to most of the logical world) that Jonathan was my bio dad.

His next email:

Hello again,

One of the reasons I am as open to helping you find your dad is that my father died when I was 6 and although I was raised by my mother, she never gave me much information about his family. I very much understand what it is like to not know about those who brought you into the world. There are so many coincidences about all this – to say nothing about the genetic match!

The problem for me right now is that I have no memory of being with anyone other than Marian Michaels during this time. I have written to her about this and asked her if she remembers any of the names you wrote about. I have not heard back yet. Also, I majored in Art and English, and although I helped teach an evening class at the city college, that lasted less than a month. I do not even remember if I took any classes at the local junior college. I was and still am an artist and I was well known for the jewelry and metal work I did. I used to sell my work at the beach every weekend. I think most people who knew me then would have connected me with art and the craft of jewelry making. The description in the paperwork you provided simply does not describe me back then. The area where I lived was very different then... many artists, writers and creative minds.

It has been a long time and you have piqued my curiosity to no end. There is so much coincidence in time place and of course the genetic info.

My Best,
Jonathan

I was happy he was open and honest and willing to help me find my dad.

Chapter Thirteen – The Truth Fears No Questions

The man who lies to the world, is the world's slave from then on…
There are no white lies, there is only the blackest of destruction,
and a white lie is the blackest of all.
~Ayn Rand, "Atlas Shrugged"

My story so far, provided to me by the esteemed Mr. Witt, San Bernardino County Social Services, was my truth. I clung to it. It was *mine*, and I believed it was all true. Margaret, a young, wanna-be hippie, started experimenting with drugs at age sixteen or seventeen. In the beginning, her hip mother and stepfather included her in their beatnik party scene, and she was flattered to be part of this group.

Margaret's experimentation with drugs quickly extended beyond pot smoking. She had a boyfriend, a couple of years older than her, who also dabbled in drugs. It was the 1960s, after all. Hell, it was her own mother (my grandmother!) who introduced Margaret to smoking pot. But, the party didn't last long. According to the story, she was arrested, along with her boyfriend (my biological father), on felony drug charges at the age of eighteen Margaret's mother, Elle, had been married to Joe since Margaret was very young. Margaret loved and respected Joe and considered him to be a fine father figure. This was all according to my truth.

Now, I was confronted with a new truth. The truth as told

to me by Jonathan Winter, my biological father. The DNA evidence could not be denied – he was definitely my father – unless he had a twin who shared his DNA, which he didn't.

But, here was the troubling part: At this point, I had been in contact with Jonathan for months via email. We'd been taking things slowly. He admitted he's an "old hippie" and he dabbled in drugs back in the 60s (some pretty powerful drugs, at that). Yes, he lived in the same town as Margaret and her family (just a few blocks away). Yes, he's the right age, *exactly*. But, the description of my biological father and the information provided to me by Mr. Witt in the non-identifying information did not describe Jonathan (according to Jonathan). From the non-identifying information:

In high school, your birth father was the editor of a literary magazine. He was also on the debate team and participated in political groups. He and your birth mother enjoyed talking about literature, intellectual subjects and attended classes together at the junior college in their community… Your birth father was also working at a pet hospital… and had access to narcotic drugs… Both of your parents were arrested on drug-related charges…. We have no record of your birth father after his arrest.

That's the birth father I thought I knew from my non-identifying information. Consider, however, that all this information was taken directly from the social services file on Margaret. All the descriptive information about what happened and who was involved was based on what Margaret told the social worker(s) when she was eighteen years old, pregnant, and in prison. Margaret told *no one* in her own family she was pregnant, so no one spoke to social workers or prison personnel about Margaret and her situation except Margaret. Margaret could have said anything. She was young, ashamed, probably scared, and being questioned and pressured for information, whilst making a life-changing decision about the baby growing inside of her. She told social workers the birthfather "didn't know [I] was pregnant, for sure." The documentation indicated that Margaret "signed sole custody relinquishments on December 20, 1963." *Sole custody*. My birth father did not know.

Or, perhaps Margaret didn't know the identity of my biological father. Maybe it could have been one of several? Or, maybe she didn't remember the encounter. Or, maybe she knew, but she decided to describe someone different to throw off the authorities. Or, me. The fact is… the information provided to me in the non-identifying information did *not* describe Jonathan Winter. And, not just by my comparison. By his own, as well.

I sent Jonathan copies of the photos I had of Margaret. I also sent him copies of the letters Margaret and I exchanged over twenty years ago (which were really no help at all, since Margaret said nothing at all about the time surrounding her pregnancy, except that it was a *handicap* that needed to be fixed). He contacted several of his long-time friends, including his old flame Marian Michaels, and told them about me and the "odd coincidences" (as he called them) of my story. No one recalled a Margaret Michaels.

Miraculously, Jonathan did not back away from me; rather, he opened up considerably and told me everything he could remember. I believed what he told me. He had absolutely no reason to hide anything. If he had a secret to hide, why would he continue to tell me his story? The odd part was that Margaret Michaels was not a part of his story. He was also never arrested, as claimed by Margaret. He was not interested in literature or politics, and he did not attend any classes at the local junior college. Jonathan and Margaret didn't even attend the same high school. Margaret had claimed my birth father was the editor of a literary magazine in high school. That was simply not true.

The story of Jonathan's life was beginning to unfold before me. We exchanged many emails over the course of several months. I was eager for information about my biological father's history, while Jonathan was trying desperately to figure out the connection and remember something… anything.

Jonathan was known for his art. He was (and still is) a jewelry maker and metal worker. He used to sell his art and jewelry at the beach in Santa Barbara every weekend. He had a small studio/shop on the corner near the beach and hung out with other artists and "creative minds," as he called them. He told me stories about how the beach community where he lived was a great artist mecca back in the 1960s. He never worked at a pet hospital. That's not where he got his drugs.

I think most people who knew me then would have connected me with art and the craft of jewelry making. It was very different then… many artists, writers and creative minds. There was a wonderful man named Bobby Hyde who owned a great deal of land and would sell it cheap to friends and other artists. He even traded land for art. One case I remember – he traded ½ an acre for an old school bus. I know that must be hard to imagine but that the land above Santa Barbara was not thought of as prime property back then. Poor artists could live there and many of them did – in houses that some of them even built themselves.

Bobby Hyde sounded like an interesting character, so I did a little research.

Bobby was a writer, artist, and reformer of sorts in the Bohemian community in the hills above Santa Barbara in Southern California in the 1940s, 50s, and 60s. He was also the unofficial founder of the nonconformist community known as *Mountain Drive*. As the story goes, Bobby would sell off parcels of his own land to friends and other artists and help them build their own family homes from handmade adobe bricks and whatever construction materials they could unearth. This was during the time before uniform building codes and laws regarding legal subdividing and building permits existed. From these humble beginnings grew a spirited artistic community. The inhabitants of the early Mountain Drive community believed in living free in their uncontrolled and unconventional society – focusing on joining together as a community family to work hard and lead pleasurable, interesting, natural and aesthetic lives.

As a direct result of the unique culture of Mountain Drive in the 1950s and 1960s, an evolution of new arts, crafts, recreation, philosophies, sciences, politics, architecture, design, community farming, cuisine, winemaking, and a whole host of other uniquely Californian ideas emerged. Call it the Bohemian beat culture or the beginning of the hippie movement – no matter what you call it, those who grew into young adults during the late 1950s and 1960s will attest to the economic, social, and cultural upheaval surrounding this period, especially in California.

Folklore would have you believe that the hippie movement started in San Francisco (everyone has heard of the *Summer of Love* in the late 1960s), but in reality, the counterculture of free thinking, artistic living, and hedonism started early in the 1960s in the Golden State in places like the hills above Santa Barbara and spread like wildfire up and down the entire coast of California.

For Santa Barbara, the movement took hold largely because of this unique environment created accidentally by Bobby Hyde and his wife, Florence (fondly known as "Floppy" to family and friends because of the large floppy hats she wore). The goings-on in the Mountain Drive community lured some of the most influential personalities of the countercultural world, including Dylan Thomas, Ken Kesey, Timothy Leary, Baba Ram Dass, Bill Neely, Frank Robinson, and many others to live, study, play, visit, and create in the hills above Santa Barbara.

Mountain Drive also became a pit stop of sorts for artists, poets, aspiring actors, musicians, and all sorts of hipsters traveling between San Francisco and Los Angeles. It was the influence of these creative minds living and playing on Mountain Drive and in the surrounding areas that cultivated the concepts, creations, and ideology that would become an integral part of what is now Santa Barbara, Montecito, and all of Southern and Central California.

Did you know that the hot tub was invented up on Mountain Drive? And, believe it or not, the Renaissance

Pleasure Faire now staged throughout the country actually originated on Mountain Drive. It all started as a "Pot War," although not like you're imagining. The local hippie artists would dress in Renaissance inspired garb and sell their handmade pottery and other art by the roadside, pouring wine into the handmade cups for the patrons as they purchased. Copious amounts of local (often homemade) wine was consumed by both the artists and the visitors. Musicians eventually joined in the fun with their guitars and recorders and entertained the growing crowds. This Pot War became the inspiration for the Renaissance Pleasure Faire when a small group of individuals who had visited the festivities in the hills above Santa Barbara decided to host a similar event near Los Angeles as a fundraiser. The Renaissance Pleasure Faire was born. Thank you (I think), Mountain Drive.

Weather permitting, clothing was optional in and around Mountain Drive. The community had its share of dedicated nudists. Gardening in the nude was commonplace. After all, the sun shone warm on the hillside nearly three hundred days per year.

Mountain Drive also became famous for its naked grape stomping parties that were held annually to celebrate the grape harvest from nearby Santa Ynez Valley. Each fall, all the families in the neighborhood would pack up their old cars with picnic feasts and harvesting supplies and make the trek over the San Marcos pass to the vineyards. The party began with the picking and didn't stop until the vines were bare, the feast was done, and the grapes were packed in wooden crates and readied for the haul back to Mountain Drive. Once back in the hippy enclave, the grapes were emptied into a large wooden vat below one of the handmade adobe homes. The men would then choose a "wine queen" from amongst the wives and other women of the Drive. The Queen would be crowned with a wreath of grape vines, and she would then lead the party goers, young and old, into the vat, *au naturel*, for the crush. Even the children were allowed to participate in the crush.

The conditions being what they were, the wine was never

really very good. In fact, a lot of it was eventually turned into vinegar. But, it was the ceremony of it all that made the wine stomp on Mountain Drive so grand. The tradition of the harvest and the annual wine stomp went on for many years. In fact, a monument to the celebration still stands in the Mountain Drive community today. At one point along the Drive, which is now paved and dotted with huge multimillion-dollar homes, you can visit a colorful fountain that was built by a local artist as a memorial to the Mountain Drive Wine Stomps. I made a pilgrimage to Mountain Drive several years ago to explore my bio dad's neighborhood and was surprised and delighted to find it. The names of the Wine Queens for each year are painted on the colorful fountain tiles. The names Bobby and Floppy Hyde can also be found engraved on stone on the fountain.

As would be expected, the parties in the hills above Santa Barbara got looser and raunchier as the years progressed. During the early 1960s and into the 1970s, the younger generation in the small, free-spirited, artistic community that had previously evolved and thrived solely on communal living and counterculture welcomed the new drug scene.

This is where Jonathan grew up. I'm grateful Jonathan has been very open with me about his youth and drug use during that time. It has helped me to understand more about my complicated origins.

Jonathan confessed that from about age fifteen to twenty-two (the late 50s and early 60s) he went through a period of rebellion, exploration, and searching for the truth, or meaning of life. He told me stories of experimentation with mescaline, LSD, and of course, marijuana, inspired by his reading of Aldous Huxley's *The Doors of Perception*. Jonathan wrote in an email:

The idea that a drug could open the mind to a spiritual world appealed to me. I sent away to a company in England and ordered one gram of mescaline sulphate. I remember my mother picking it up at the post office and asking me what it was. I think I told her it had something to do with my art… I don't really remember. But that was my first experience with any drug more potent than marijuana.

Mail order drugs. *Wow.* Who knew? Jonathan also wrote to me about some of his artist friends from the area.

The artists and writers I knew were good people and had successful lives… at least from my perspective. Several of them are still good friends. Dale Pendell, a Buddhist and poet and I are still the best of friends. In fact, I called him and asked if he might remember Margaret or any of the names you provided. None rang a bell for him.

Another clue? On his website, Dale Pendell is described as a contemporary poet, author, and expert on pharmacology, ethnobotany, and neuroscience. *Pharmacology? Ethnobotany?* Dale died in 2018. He was obviously an intelligent, thoughtful man, but I'm not so sure I would have trusted his memory.

The information on his website touched on his general beliefs and also listed his published works. His message revolved around what he called "earth-centered living" and an acknowledgment that we are all part of a great living fabric, and that plants, animals, and even certain sacred places are endowed with a spiritual presence, or energy. All of his beliefs somehow tied into the psychedelic revolution that blossomed in the 1960s. He wrote his first book, *Gold Dust Wilderness*, in 1970. He had this to say about writing that first book (from his website, dalependell.com):

My first book was written while living in a tiny cabin at Flores Flats in the mountains above Santa Barbara in 1970. It is a book of haibun of my life on a mining claim on the North Fork of the Trinity River between 1967 and 1970, and illustrated with pictographs and petroglyphs. It's a hand-made book, printed by silk-screen process in a small garage in Santa Barbara, and hand bound using flexible sewing while Jon Winter and his wife fed me and let me sleep in their yard. I printed a hundred and fifty copies, washing out the screens as I went along.

Later, Jonathan told me how he remembered the pages from Dale's book strung from the rafters in his garage to dry. He showed me one of the original copies of the book, which he still treasures. The poetry is stark but meaningful. The art is primitive but pleasing.

Those groovy 1960s. What a decade, right? The pharmaceutical industry exploded with research into new drugs. Drugs were legally developed for every illness, disorder and disease. Thanks to the legal drug industry's aggressive media campaigns, every medicine cabinet filled up with drugs for every sort of ailment, real and imagined. The phrase "better living through chemistry" came from a legitimate DuPont advertisement. Drugs were portrayed as wonders of modern technology. In the early 1960s, drugs were not seen as evil. So, of course, young people, as young people want to do, experimented. Luckily for Jonathan, it was all a positive experience. Except for one thing: he believed his drug use was the reason he lost the love of his life – Marian Michaels.

He and Marian attended the Laguna Blanca School, a private high school in Santa Barbara (*not* the same high school that Margaret attended). They met when she was fourteen and he was sixteen. She was one grade below him in school. They fell in love as teenagers. Jonathan told me the sweet story of their young love. Jonathan's drug use continued into his late teens (and escalated), and this is where the problem started between Jonathan and Marian. I believe that Jonathan was being completely honest with me when he wrote to me about his drug use:

I went on a walk up into the hills above Santa Barbara determined to find the "answer" and took the drug. Now what is interesting here, at least to me, is that during this time there was nothing much known or written about the negative possibilities of taking such a substance. I had only positive expectations and ended up having the experience of a lifetime.

It is hard to describe but I became one with all things. I could see and feel the connection I had to creation.

I won't go on, but suffice it to say that this first time experience stays with me to this day…. and in a positive way. It was as though it set my mind to understand the connection we all have to the universe and to all things.

The sad part to all this was that because of my drug use I broke the trust which I had built with Marian. I was no longer the person she had grown to love.

Jonathan explained that once he realized Marian was drifting away from him because of the drug use, he "went into the mountains" and stayed there for several months until he was "no longer addicted." But, when he returned home, it was too late. Marian had moved on. She eventually married and had two children. Jonathan also eventually married and had a daughter.

Later communication with Jonathan revealed what "into the mountains" may have meant:

You were born when I was 20 and looking back at that time I was in Big Sur living and working at Deetjen's Big Sur Inn. I think I had started working there sometime in 1962…… at least I have a few photos of me there which are dated 1962.

My math indicates that I was conceived in April 1963 (born mid-December, one month premature. Jonathan's a little fuzzy on exactly where he was at that time.

While Jonathan and I were working our way through the details via email, he had indicated a desire to submit DNA to a different company (or resubmit to *23andMe* under another name) and to ask his daughter (who was thirty-seven years old at the time) to also submit a sample to see what kind of a match would be revealed between the three of us. I understood his trepidation, but let's be real: DNA doesn't lie. I believed he was my biological father. He was still not so sure.

Laureen, I want you to know that I would be proud to have you as my daughter. I have no negative feelings but I am very confused about all of this. It seems so unlikely that our DNA would be so close and then the connection to Santa Barbara where I grew up…

What I would really like to do is talk to Margaret… That would settle things…

Even back then I doubt I would have been drawn to someone like that. All of the women that I had any relationships with (there were not many) I still know and we are still friends, including Marian.

I provided him with the address I had for Margaret. He told me that he had started to write a letter to her several times, but he could not finish. He wanted to say just the right thing. I knew the feeling.

Chapter Fourteen – Rewriting the Past

The self is not something one finds, it is something one creates.
~Thomas Szasz

I had answers to some of the most basic, vital questions. I knew the identity of my biological mother: Margaret Michaels.

I knew the identity of my biological father (thanks to DNA): Jonathan Winter.

The last contact I had with Margaret was the self-bloated letter I received from her over twenty years earlier. She still had no desire to meet me or to even carry on a conversation via letter or email. I have honored that request (although "honor" doesn't really seem like the right word).

The only people in her world who knew she was pregnant and relinquished a child were the prison personnel (and presumably other inmates), social workers, and hospital personnel. It is also possible that her stepfather knew. According to the report from the investigator, from the prison or arrest records she was able to uncover, he was the one who turned Margaret in to the authorities, which resulted in her arrest. Perhaps Margaret's stepfather was doing what he could to protect her baby. If Margaret were incarcerated, she most likely couldn't continue any drug use.

But was it true that none of Margaret's family came to visit her during her incarceration? What a sad thought. She was there for nearly four years (sentenced to ten). I suppose if anyone had come to see her during the first three months of her stay, they would have surely guessed she was pregnant (or thought she really liked the prison food). I suppose that if she had visitors after December, they would not have known she had ever been pregnant. She gave birth right before Christmas. No one visited her over the holidays?

It made sense that Margaret's mother, Elle (my grandmother) wouldn't come to see her early on during her incarceration. She had her hands full with three small children and a newborn. Elle was pregnant *at the same time as Margaret.* Remember this from my non-identifying story?

Baby Christian is the 3-month old half brother.

Elle gave birth to Baby Christian (my uncle) about the same time Margaret was arrested. And, it was Baby Christian's father (Margaret's stepfather) who turned Margaret in to the authorities, according to the story cobbled together with my non-identifying information.

Jonathan obviously didn't know Margaret was pregnant. Jonathan claimed he didn't remember Margaret Michaels *at all.* Drugs can alter memories, for sure. But, Jonathan did remember *Marian* Michaels. His first love. He's still in touch with her some fifty years later. Jonathan even told Marian about me and our curious DNA match and about this mysterious Margaret person who has the same last name as Marian. According to Jonathan, Marian was not able to provide any information that would be helpful to us.

I was still in touch with Joannie, Margaret's half-sister, via email. At one point, we discussed getting together to meet and talk. Unlike Margaret, she seemed genuinely interested in getting to know me. I was hopeful that she could fill in some of the odd-shaped blanks hanging out there. She was very clear that Margaret did not want to discuss the matter and did not want to be involved in any contact with me. She also confirmed that their mother, Elle, still did not know about me. And, she was *not* going to tell her.

It was about this time that I started blogging about my journey to discover my adoption truth to help me sort through it all. Joannie read the blog. She sent me an email expressing her disappointment with the information I was putting out there in the cyber-world for anyone to see (even though I had changed the names of the key players). She asked me to take the information down, claiming that some of the details provided to me in the non-identifying information were "untrue." She felt it was an invasion of her family's privacy.

I was taken aback. *Not true?* You mean the story that I know and live every day about my identity and how I came into this world is riddled with untruths, cover-ups, and lies? Imagine that. *I've lived this way my entire life.*

Before I started writing the blog, Joannie had asked me to share the information I had discovered about my biological father through the DNA match. She wanted to know what I had learned about my biological father. I believed she was sympathetic to my plight and genuinely interested. Without hesitation, I told her about the surprise DNA match and gave details that Jonathan had shared with me, in the hopes that sharing the information with Margaret's sister may lead to more sharing on her side of the family. I responded carefully, but honestly:

Hi Joannie,

I am sorry that you are uncomfortable with the story unfolding on the blog. It's not about making my story better; I'm simply telling it. For over 25 years, I've had bits and pieces of information, along with several "holes" in my life story that I have never been able to explain. Frankly, I'm tired of hearing the phrase "invasion of privacy." Opening up the truth to uncover secrets and lies that have been kept for a lifetime at someone else's expense is certainly not an invasion of privacy in my book. As I begin filling in these holes, I feel the need to put it all in writing. It's like I'm rewriting my past. A past that I didn't have or wasn't entitled to.

I believe it is important to share my journey – I want other adoptees to know what may be available to them in their search for their own truth. Responses and feedback I have received tell me I'm doing the right thing.

I understood Margaret's family owed me nothing. And, I considered that perhaps Margaret was bullying her siblings into not communicating with me. From what I understood, they were worried that the knowledge of my existence would have a negative effect emotionally on their mother (my grandmother, Elle). I wondered what, exactly, could be so devastating about my mere existence that it would emotionally crush my grandmother? The fact that Margaret had a child? No, that couldn't be. At that point in Margaret's life, who cared if she had a child? That child was all grown up now. And seriously, I hadn't lived the kind of life that could be deemed a disappointment to anyone, in my own humble opinion.

It had to be the fifty-year-old lie. It had to be that her daughter, Margaret, never told her she had a child. Surely, she knew that Margaret had been in prison. That "disappointment" had already been felt, processed, and dealt with, I would assume. Or, who knew? Perhaps, there was more to the story that I didn't know. Margaret's sister wrote:

We do not know the circumstances leading to her pregnancy; it may have been quite traumatic.

Absent the truth, I wrote my own story.

Adoptees, for the most part, are natural storytellers. We never really had a choice. Adoptees are wired to explain – we explain our lives, our families, our histories (as much as we know or make up) from the beginning. At first, we retell the stories that are given to us – the stories of being "chosen" and "special." Things *they* told us, like, *"As soon as I saw you, I knew you were mine."*

But, those stories are often not enough. Most adoptees fill in their bare-bones stories with fantasies. Every adoptee I have ever met has confessed to fantasizing at some point about his or her unknown parents and families. The fantasies usually begin when a child first understands they were given away and asks, "*Why did it happen? Who are they? Where are they now? Do they think about me?*" The fantasies are natural and inevitable. When you don't know about something that demands explanation, you make it up. This sort of storytelling has been going on for centuries.

Not just for adoptees. Ancient mythology and mythological creatures were created by reasonable and intelligent adult human beings as a way to explain the unknown and create order in a chaotic, untamed world. In ancient civilizations, fantastic imaginary creatures using magic and superhuman powers were often the answer to rather fundamental questions before religion, philosophy, and science allowed us to find or get closer to the actual truth.

For example, how would you explain something as simple as the changing of the seasons and the weather patterns before science? Simple. Enter Persephone, the sweet and beautiful mythical daughter of the Greek goddess Demeter (goddess of vegetation and the harvest), who was kidnapped by Hades (the infamous and feared god of the Underworld). Demeter is so heartbroken because of her sadness over losing her daughter, she does not allow anything to grow on earth – no flowers, no trees, and no food crops. The earth becomes a wasteland. Zeus (he's the boss-god) is not happy with the harsh environment created by the absence of Persephone, so he demands Hades return Persephone to her mother. Hades strikes a deal with Zeus – Persephone would be returned only if she has not eaten any food from the underworld (this seems odd, but… okay). Well, wouldn't you know it? It turns out Persephone had eaten six pomegranate seeds while she was in the underworld. (Only six? That's weird. I love pomegranates – it would be impossible for me to eat only six seeds.)

As the story goes, it is decided that for six months out of the year, Persephone will be allowed to live with her mother on earth, but for the other six months of the year – one month for every seed she ate – she will be forced to live in the underworld with Hades. The six months that Persephone is on earth are, of course, spring and summer. Demeter is so happy to have her daughter back for those six months that she allows all the flowers and plants to bloom and grow. During the fall and winter, when Persephone is back in the underworld with Hades, the plants die, leaves fall off the trees, and the weather becomes cold and harsh.

Adoptee fantasies, like myths, are a way of explaining that for which there is no explanation. The contrived fantasies invented by adoptees have authority and usefulness not by proving themselves as true, but as comforting mechanisms for a questioning, troubled mind.

All my older brother, Tommy, knew about his origins was that he was born in Hollywood. Imagine how that single fact might morph into a storybook-type fantasy about a beautiful, young starlet mother and a handsome, movie-star father. When I was a young girl, I imagined that once Tommy's beautiful starlet birth mother made the *Big Time* in Hollywood, she might come to claim him and take him away from us. At times I had hoped for it. Then, he'd become famous and have a great life because of this fantasy-woman's fame and stardom. At the time, I was even jealous of the fantasy that I had created for him. It was way more interesting and fairy-tale-like than my prison baby truth and fantasy about a drug-addicted mother who couldn't take care of me.

But, alas, the movie-star mom never came to claim Tommy.

As adoptees get older, we may shed the fantasies, but we still wonder. There are still questions. Some of us are drawn to search for the truth. Others decide that leaving certain questions unasked is what will allow us to find peace. Not me.

Chapter Fifteen – Sisterhood

Love, Mercy, and Grace, sisters all,
attend your wounds of silence and hope.
~Aberjhani, "The River of Winged Dreams"

Even though my older adopted brother, Tommy, and I grew up in the same household with the same parents, I've always had difficulty thinking of him as my brother. He's my family and I love him, but family is such a weird thing for adoptees. My brother and I are *so* different. So far apart in personality, thoughts, interests and goals. It may seem cliché to say, but we really didn't – and still don't – have a single thing in common.

Of course, there is the obvious – we don't look alike at all. He was a red-headed kid with freckles, gawky and uncoordinated. I had olive skin, dark brown hair and eyes – similar to our adoptive parents. I don't know if it ever bothered him that I looked like our mom and dad and he didn't. We never really talked about that. He was, however, two years older than me, and when we were kids, he could beat me at just about everything – like fake Kung Fu fighting in the living room and running a race while dribbling a basketball in the backyard. He was stronger than me and could also push me around. Which he did often. It was just normal sibling stuff. I don't hold any of it against him.

I do remember, however, feeling a huge triumph when I discovered I could skip with ease across the backyard before I was five years old. Tommy never learned to skip. I made a point to break into a happy skip whenever I could in front of him so that he could see me do it.

I was even more proud when I managed to master the use of chopsticks while on a family vacation in San Francisco one summer. My parents were impressed when I plucked the sweet and sour chicken from the giant platter without much effort and tossed it in my mouth at the tender age of eight. Tommy was ten at the time and struggled to just hold both chopsticks in one hand. Even the waitress joined in and was fussing, along with my parents, over my achievement with the awkward wooden utensils. As I beamed with pride at the adoration and at finding another thing I could do better than my older brother, Tommy began to cry right there in the restaurant in China Town. I didn't feel sorry for him. I gloated. My parents even allowed me to get my ears pierced the very next day. It was the best vacation ever.

I considered my two best friends to be my sisters. To this day, they are still like sisters to me. Or, as I imagine sisters would be. We live far apart now – I'm here in California while Debbie and her family are in Arizona, and Nancy is raising her brood near Chicago – but because we shared so much growing up, I feel a lifelong bond that must be like sisterhood. We spent so much time with each other and each other's families, it feels like one big happy family to me in a lot of ways. I know about their secrets, disappointments, conflicts, and ongoing disputes within their families. I feel as comfortable with all of it as I do with my own family issues.

Both Debbie and Nancy have older biological sisters. I've always wondered how their relationships with me differ from their sisters-in-blood. I know Nancy's older sister, Sandy, didn't care for me all that much when we were growing up. She thought I tried too hard to be like Nancy. I think it had a lot to do with the genetic mirroring I had missed out on. I recognize now that sometimes I would latch on to people that I liked and try to emulate the things in them that I admired. Nancy didn't seem to mind. Maybe Sandy was jealous of my closeness with

Nancy.

What was so weird about the situation with Sandy was that, during her teen years, she became friends with a group of Hispanic or Latina girls and tried desperately to become one of them. She mirrored their severe make-up, the plucked thin brows, extreme feathered hair (big wings, as we used to call them), and the creased bell bottom pants (this was the late 70s). She even mimicked their Mexican accent and used their slang. Nancy and I thought it was ridiculous. She was trying to be something she wasn't. Her blonde hair was a dead giveaway, but her friends didn't seem to mind.

Now I knew I had a biological sister of my own. Jonathan's daughter, Megan, is thirteen years younger than me. She is Jonathan's only other child. I wondered if she might be interested in getting to know her half-sister from California.

I introduced myself in a letter I sent to Megan via email. By this time, I had been communicating with Jonathan for several months.

February 7, 2014

Hi Megan,

My name is Laureen Pittman. You probably already know who I am. I assume that your father, Jonathan, has told you about me and our surprising, yet remarkable DNA match through 23andMe. It was nothing but absolute pure luck that I found him. I feel happy and more whole knowing who my biological father is, and I am hopeful I can find a place in his life without disrupting his family life as he knows it and the love, order and harmony that apparently already exists within him.

As you probably know, Jonathan and I had been communicating via email for several months, beginning last August. He was so open and honest with me – I appreciated it so much. We formed a friendship of sorts – I know he was skeptical about our DNA match and did not want to believe that he had fathered a child back in 1963 – he has no memory of my biological mother. It's a complicated story, but I was (and still am) so touched and grateful that he was willing to communicate with me and let me into his life, even if only on a "virtual" level. I believe that he knows in his heart that he is my father (there can be no other explanation for the DNA match and the "coincidences" of time and place so many years ago), but with his memory of the events that happened more than 50 years ago being "fuzzy," perhaps he is afraid of who I am or my intentions.

I'll give you a little bit of background, so you don't think I'm some crazy stalker (maybe it's too late for that!). Anyway, I am 50 years old and I have known all of my life that I was adopted. I will spare you the details and just say that I am a happy, well-adjusted adult and I harbor no anger or resentment toward my adoptive family or my biological parents. I located my biological mother many years ago and unfortunately, we have never been able to make an emotional connection. She has never wanted to know me, or even know of me. I have respected her wishes. We have never met nor do we carry on any kind of ongoing communication. She has made it clear that it is her opinion that any contact from me would upset her and her immediate family greatly. I am sad about that, and while I don't understand her reasoning, I have respected her wishes and have reached a place of peace knowing I will never know her or have her in my life. That was over 20 years ago.

I turned to 23andme just last year to take advantage of their health analysis reports – identifying family traits and predicting possible congenital risk factors for diseases – since I had no family "history" to reference. I'm finding as I get older, I have more and more questions about my health, not only for me, but for my children. As for finding my biological father, I thought it would be a great bonus if I found some connection to him, but I didn't have much hope in that regard. As far as I knew, my biological mother was the only person on this planet that knew the identity of my biological father and she wasn't talking. But then, to my utter amazement, 23andme found my father: Jonathan.

I initially contacted Jonathan through 23andme. He was quite surprised, but open and happy to communicate with me and tell me what he could remember. We continue to communicate via e-mail. I've shared quite a bit of personal information with him, hoping something would stir his memory.

I hope Jonathan will continue communicating with me and perhaps build a relationship with me and my family. I would love to hear from you, as well, and perhaps build a relationship, if you are willing.

I look forward to hearing from you soon.

Yours,
Laureen

Chapter Sixteen – Real Life

*We should not be so taken up in the search for truth,
as to neglect the duties of active life; for it is only action
that gives a true value and commendation to virtue.*
~Marcus Tullius Cicero

Megan never responded to me directly. I was disappointed. She did share my message with Jonathan, though. Shortly after I sent the message to Megan, I learned Jonathan was trying to reach me via Facetime and Skype.

My husband, Guy, and I were already in bed, allowing the flicker of the television and the drone of the ten o'clock news lull us to sleep.

"Mom! What's your dad's name?" That woke me up. I lifted my head from the pillow as my son, Garrett, then fourteen years old, rounded the corner and burst into our bedroom, iPhone in hand.

"Garrett," I mumbled, "you're supposed to be getting ready for bed. School tomorrow. Turn your phone off."

"What's your dad's name?" he demanded.

"You know grandpa's name: Hank. Did you brush your teeth?"

"No, your *biological* dad. Is it John?"

"Jonathan."

"Jonathan Winter?"

"Yes. Why?" I was still groggy.

"I think he's been trying to FaceTime me."

"No, he *hasn't*. Garrett, I'm tired—"

"Yes, he has! Like three times in the last week." Garrett was poking at his phone like teenagers do. "I kept ignoring it cuz I didn't recognize the number, and I thought it was some sales call or something. He tried about an hour ago… and it just hit me who it was!" He was still poking.

"Why would he be trying to FaceTime you?" I was sitting straight up in bed by this time. So was Guy.

"I don't know – he must be trying to get ahold of you." Garrett poked his phone one last time and handed it to me as it started to ring.

"Crap! What are you *doing*!?" I shrieked as I took the phone from him. "I can't talk to him right now! I'm in bed! This is weird! I'm not prepared!" I was poking like hell trying to disconnect the call.

Then, I saw his face on the tiny screen. "Hello!" It was a strange voice, but somehow familiar.

I continued communicating with Jonathan, mostly via email. He still asked questions and still wanted to know more about Margaret. I wish I knew more. He had written a few letters to Margaret, but he never sent them.

Jonathan still wanted to re-submit his DNA to confirm our father/daughter match. I was fine with that, so I told him to let me know how and when he wanted to approach it. I thought it would be a good idea to submit samples from both of my boys at the same time. Perhaps, a double dose of grandson matches would convince him beyond a reasonable doubt he was my biological father.

A few months earlier, when Jonathan originally suggested sending in another sample, he mentioned getting Megan to submit a sample. I thought it was a good idea, too, if it would give him some assurance the DNA match was not a mistake. But, apparently, Megan was not interested. It was becoming obvious she wasn't interested in developing a relationship with her biological half-sister since she never responded to my message. That's okay. These things take time. And, I knew from experience that you just can't rush (or force) these things.

Chapter Seventeen – The Grandfather Clause

*The two hardest tests on the spiritual road are the patience
to wait for the right moment and the courage not to be
disappointed with what we encounter.*
~Paulo Coelho

I used to be a paralegal. I spent nearly twenty years with my
nose in law books – mostly the tax code – researching,
analyzing, planning, figuring, and writing. One thing is constant
about the tax code: change. Every year, there would be some
sort of reform – cuts, new provisions or regulations, limit
changes, incentives, exemptions, inflation adjustments – and I
had to stay on top of it. And, often, there was a sneaky
grandfather clause.

The good ol' *grandfather clause.* The exception to the rule.
Sometimes, when new laws or regulations are enacted and
imposed, a grandfather clause is an exception given to
individuals (or businesses), allowing them to continue to
operate under an old law or regulation. What's old is new.
What's new doesn't apply.

Well, guess what was new here? It was confirmed! Garrett
and Zach had a living, biological grandfather! This was a
different kind of grandfather clause, for sure.

Jonathan never got around to deciding where or when to
submit a new test for himself or for me. So, I submitted the

boys' saliva in 2014 to *23andMe*.

The results confirmed that Garrett and Zachary were half-brothers and Jonathan was their grandfather (no surprise again, at least to me).

I shared the news with the boys. They were nonplussed. They didn't know Jonathan, except for what I had been able to tell them. I wrote an email to Jonathan:

April 2014

Hi Jonathan,

Hope all is well with you. Last time we communicated, you had just turned 71! I hope you're kicking 71's ass and keeping busy with your art and the Museum. I'd love to see any new work you've completed.

We've been busy with baseball – Garrett's team was undefeated for the season – first place! And now he's on the All-Star team! He also just finished his science project at school and he did his presentation at the Science Fair yesterday. His project was in the top five for Life Sciences! Straight A's this year – we're so proud! His 8th grade promotion is in a couple of weeks. I can't believe my baby will be in high school next school year.

Zach has moved back home temporarily. His roommate in Los Angeles flaked out on him and he couldn't afford the rent on his own. He's looking to get back out to Hollywood or L.A. ASAP. He's still working on his music and has a lot recorded. It's a tough business to be in.

I just wanted to check in and let you know that I'm thinking about you. I also wanted to let you know I got the DNA Relative results of Zachary and Garrett's 23andMe tests. I don't know if you're still getting e-mail notices from 23andMe, but you've definitely got 2 new confirmed grandsons!

I hope I'm not overwhelming you once again with too much information. I just need to tie up this journey that we're on.

Speaking of journeys, I'd like to plan a trip to the community where you and Margaret and Marian grew up. I want to spend some time in Santa Barbara to do a little research at the library and I'd love to just walk around. I'll stay in touch and share what I find, if you're okay with it.

Yours,
Laureen

I was relieved that it didn't take Jonathan too long to respond:

Hi there, Laureen,

It is good to hear all is well with you and you are able to help Zach. It is a difficult world for the younger ones today; I see so many qualified (in their field of study, talent or interest) who are trying to find work that is fulfilling and will bring in enough for a good life.

Jonathan didn't acknowledge the news about having two grandsons, but it was comforting to me that he acknowledged Zach's endeavors and struggles. He talked about his daughter, whose family shared his home, as well.

I find that having my daughter's family living here to be wonderful. As long as I am not living in the same space it is a joy to have them all part of my life.

Slowly, I was getting to know my biological father. He was a man of many creative talents, great curiosity and remarkable intelligence. In addition to his unique metalworking art and jewelry-making, he is the founder and curator of the Spark Museum of Electrical Invention in Bellingham, Washington. A real, legitimate museum. Spark is a non-profit, interactive museum for education and science, displaying some of the most significant electronic, radio, and other sound and wireless inventions and innovations that literally changed how we communicate and connect. That cell phone that you're holding in your hand? Jonathan can tell you about the origins of the wireless technology that gave birth to it. The collections at the

Spark Museum, a substantial amount of which was collected and donated by Jonathan, include some of the most significant items of their kind in the world.

For Jonathan, the museum started with an interest in radios when he was just a boy. Before he started making jewelry and exploring his artistic side, he loved taking things apart, especially radios, figuring out how they worked and putting them back together again. He would find old junk radios and hunt for spare or discarded parts and tinker with them. Jonathan became fascinated with antique radios and the evolution of wireless sound travel. Eventually, he started collecting.

By 1985, Jonathan, with his wife, Judith, and their little girl, Megan, had left sunny Santa Barbara and moved to Washington State. He continued with his art and was also working with a company he co-founded that built and installed large broadcast satellite dishes for residential television. Jonathan and his business partner worked in the satellite business in rural Washington State during the early days of the satellite television industry and did very well. He still tinkered with his growing collection of radios and related electronics. The collection grew to the point of needing to be sorted out and organized.

Eventually, Jonathan brought together his formidable collection of radio sets, spare parts, schematics, recordings, and vintage magazines and manuals and set up a display in a small storefront in downtown Bellingham, Washington. By 1998, the *Bellingham Antique Radio Museum* was officially established. The museum took on the name *American Museum of Radio and Electricity* in 2001 when it moved into a 23,000-square-foot building, and John Jenkins, a former sales and marketing executive at Microsoft, teamed up with Jonathan and they became co-curators of the museum. Jenkins added his collection of early wireless and electrical devices to the museum, and the *SPARK Museum of Electrical Invention* was born. The museum currently features unique and rare artifacts showcasing four centuries of human innovation in electricity and communication from 1580 into the 1950s.

I feel a genuine sense of pride when he talks about his museum and his art.

The Museum is doing well… in fact, over this holiday we had the largest number of visitors to date. Sunday saw over 160 paying visitors with 70 watching the electric show. This was a big day for the Museum.

I have put some of my art and jewelry in a rather odd place. I found a little bead shop run by a woman who has spent much of her life collecting primitive art and antique beads from around the world. She is in her early 80's and does not wear shoes most of the time… a real character, but very smart and happens to sell her stuff to collectors and people who appreciate the hand work and labor it takes to make such items. At any rate, I put some of my work there, and within a week I sold three masks and two silver containers for $4,000.00 to two people. This got the creative juices flowing again. I have not been very creative in the past month or so. I'm looking forward to getting back to the bench.

About my plan to make a trip to Santa Barbara:

I haven't been there in years. The street and the home where I grew up looks very different, I am sure. Until I was five the street I lived on was a small dirt road. If you do cruise up there and if Franceschi Park is open, have a look. It was my playground when I was very young. I remember being able to pick fresh guavas, and other wonderful fruit that at the time were not in the stores. Mr. Franceschi brought many of the rare trees to Santa Barbara himself. The park was where he lived and worked. He was a very old man when I lived there as a child.

Things have changed a great deal. I don't think I would recognize some of the places now, although I just used Google Earth and their "Street View" to take a look at Mission Ridge and Franceschi Rd. I was surprised at what I did remember. There are so many new homes all over the ridge…. I never would have thought it would turn out like that. The area, although there were some big houses…. it looks so covered with buildings. Yet I am sure it is heaven for those living there now.

I hope you enjoy your trip. You have my cell number, so if you want to call about anything about the area when you are there, I am happy to tell you what I can.

Well, that's it from here… I hope you have a good trip to SB….keep me posted.

Keep well and my best to you and yours,
Jonathan

Chapter Eighteen – The Tale That Never Ends

[E]verybody's life, I believe, is a kind of detective story,
every clue of our forbearers' lives, every decision, missed opportunity,
guessed motivation, a part of the solution to our own existence.
~Robin Hemley

All this time, I had been working on piecing together my own story. Along the way, however, I learned it is not only the adoptee who may have a need to fill in the blanks or rewrite the past.

Imagine a seventy-year-old ex-hippie learning for the first time via email that he has a fifty-year-old daughter. His mind was blown. Mine, too. But, why did he have his DNA tested? He wasn't looking for me. He didn't even know I existed.

I asked Jonathan that question. He explained to me at the time that he wanted to try to learn more about his own father. His mother, Millie, was forty-one when he was born in 1943, her first and only child. Jonathan's father died when he was only six years old. Poor Millie. She was trying to raise a free-spirited, artistic, rebellious child and teen in the late 1950s and early 1960s as a single mother. And, she was old enough to be his grandmother.

According to Jonathan, he and his mother were never close. She never spoke much about his father, which confused Jonathan. The only thing she would tell him was that his father was an engineer who had worked on the Golden Gate Bridge.

Even as Jonathan grew older and would ask questions about him, she never gave him any significant details about his dad. He grew to resent her for that. In her later years, Jonathan moved Millie from Santa Barbara to Washington to be close to him and his family. Millie died in 1990. On her deathbed, even as Jonathan pleaded, he says that he was not able to get any relevant information from her about his father. She would tell him repeatedly that he was so wanted and loved, thinking that would pacify and appease him. It was not enough.

As Jonathan approached the age of seventy, it occurred to him that it might be a good idea to invest in a DNA test to get some information about any potential health concerns. He had a daughter and a granddaughter to think about. And, if he got lucky, he could find out some information about his family tree and his father. Jonathan spit into a *23andMe* tube. I'm so glad he did.

I'm here to tell you, even if you don't get that jackpot close family match – like I did when I found Jonathan – if you're looking for someone specific or a specific connection, or even if you're just curious about your family tree and it seems you're hitting dead ends, stay the course with the DNA testing results and make contact with those distant relatives because you never know what will evolve. Someone out there knows your truth. They may not even know they know, and you may not think these distant relatives can provide you with any useful information, but you never know when you will get that little sliver of information that makes all the other random information come together and start to make sense. You can only put together the whole puzzle when you have all the smaller, odd-shaped pieces.

Of course, I am talking about the family puzzle. Families are the cornerstone of life, providing biological (for most) and social continuity for individuals as they also shape and are shaped by the larger society as a whole.

Society is a big factor in the shaping of a family. Adoptees experience first-hand how a society's larger agenda and values, such as attitudes toward unwed mothers and children born out of wedlock, can affect a family. Adoption itself is shaped by these values and continues to evolve as society and the idea of the American family change with the social and economic ebbs and tides of the past, present, and future.

There continue to be other factors shaping the design and structure of American families. These days, families come in all shapes and sizes. Single moms (sometimes on purpose and without shame), single dads, two moms, two dads, children being raised by grandparents, aunts, uncles, etc. The possibilities are endless. And, for the most part, families today are not bending over backward to force the appearance of a traditional, nuclear family (mom, dad, and a couple of kiddos). That was part of the problem with families back in the 1940s, 1950s, 1960s, and even into the 1970s and 80s. Often, there was what may have been considered an *oops* in a family (like premarital sex and pregnancy, or perhaps an extramarital affair that resulted in a pregnancy) and a scramble to cover it up, deny it, or re-shape it into something more acceptable or more conventional.

Cover-ups, lies, deception. Let's face it: we lie to protect ourselves. We lie to *promote* ourselves. We lie to elevate ourselves. We lie to excuse ourselves. I've said it before and I'll say it again, when a lie is told or a truth is hidden about the identity of another human being, that lie, cover-up, or informational void should not follow that person for his or her entire life. It's not right. It's just not fair.

A few weeks after Jonathan and I discovered our match on *23andMe*, I got one of those seemingly random contact emails from a 2nd-3rd cousin through the DNA Relative section of *23andMe*. He asked the usual questions, using a template provided by 23andMe:

Hi,

Through our shared DNA, 23andMe has identified us as relatives. Our predicted relationship is 2nd Cousin. Would you like to compare our genomes? By sharing genomes we can compare our DNA using ancestry features and discover clues about how we are related. Surnames in my family: Mann, Bailey, Sachse. I live in Northern California now, and I'm in my late 50s. This is my first experience with 23andMe – interesting!

Andy Mann

Well, none of those names meant anything to me, but, then again, I simply didn't know. I shared my long, sordid story with Andy. I told him about being adopted, and I told him everything I knew about Margaret's side of the family. I also told him about the crazy good luck of finding Jonathan and gave him Jonathan's full name: Jonathan Winter. Maybe, something would click with him.

Andy wrote back right away to let me know none of the names or locations rang a bell with him. No surprise. I didn't hear from Andy for several months. And then, this:

October 2014

Hi Laureen,

Have you been in touch with Jonathan Winter? My 88-year-old mom, who lives in Northern California, recently wrote me this (below). Can you forward it to him? Hope you're doing well.

– Andy Mann

From my mom:
Jonathan is the son of my Uncle Richard, your grandfather's older brother who had come to this country before your grandfather. Richard Sachse was married to Katherine and had 2 children: Franz and Marybeth. The family lived in Fallbrook, California and every Christmas would send a large box of goodies to our family: oranges, grapefruit and avocados, and always a lovely gift for me and my sister. Living in those days many miles apart, I believe I only saw him once when the family drove to Southern California when I was very young.

I do remember attending the World's Fair in San Francisco in 1915 with Uncle Richard and the rest of my family. I next spent time with Uncle Richard during WWII when I was a secretary in the Bay Area. He had an apartment on Telegraph Hill near Coit Tower because he traveled to the Bay Area for work quite often. He also maintained his home in Southern California where he would go on the weekends.

After the war, I lost track of what Uncle Richard was doing. I know he was summoned to Washington, D.C. by President Truman and made several trips to the capitol and overseas to help with post-war reparations in Europe and rebuilding.

It wasn't until I was married that I learned Uncle Richard had had an affair while married to his first wife, Katherine. Of course, everything was very hush hush. He and Katherine eventually divorced and the "other woman," whose name was Millie, had a child.

Heide

Jonathan had been looking for information about his father and had been doing bits of research via the Internet, contacting several companies where he believed his father had worked. From what he remembered from bits of information his mother told him, his father traveled quite a bit and was an engineer who had worked on the bridges in the Bay Area, including the Golden Gate Bridge. Jonathan's birth certificate identified his father as *Carl Robert Winter*, age forty-four at the time of Jonathan's birth. Also listed on the birth certificate was his father's occupation: Engineer, working for the U.S. Government in Washington, D.C. Jonathan's birth certificate also indicated Carl Robert Winter was born in San Francisco and had lived there all his life.

The engineering and construction companies he had contacted in the Bay Area were not responding to Jonathan's requests for information. It turns out that was because no one knew who Carl Robert Winter was. No such person existed in their records.

Had Millie falsified Jonathan's birth certificate? And, if so, *why the deception?*

I forwarded Andy and Heide's messages to Jonathan. I was eager for him to unlock his past and excited at what his reaction might be. It meant he'd have to look at his parents through a different lens – based on Heide's story, Jonathan's father cheated on his first wife with his mother, and Jonathan was a product of their affair. I didn't think that information would devastate him or even alarm him, especially after what he had discovered about me.

It looked to me like Jonathan and I were kindred spirits of sorts. Isn't the truth a lovely thing? And, Heide? She was so eager to help us find our identities. Heide and I eventually got in touch directly. She was so genuinely happy to have been able to help Jonathan discover the real identity of his father. She was fascinated by my story, too.

November 2014:

Laureen:

As you know, I've been in touch with your father. And, I am so very happy to give him what information I can about his father – your grandfather – and will continue to do so.

I am just sorry I'm not better informed. He said in his last email that he has shared with you what information I have given him. If you have any questions, please don't hesitate to ask, though I may very well not know the answers. Unfortunately, there are no relatives left who are old enough to provide much information. The important thing is that you have found your father! I look forward to seeing the file he is putting together. I did not know his mother and only learned of his existence shortly before your grandfather died in 1949. And I thought he was just a baby then.

As I told you, I am 88 and unfortunately losing my eyesight at an alarming rate. I have several boxes of photos to go through (I never was organized enough to put them in albums) and some of the photos belonged to my parents and some to another brother of your grandfather's, Gerhard Sachse. I was the executor of Gerhard's will. He lived in Hemet, California, by the way, but died in early 1980s. That is where I found

Richard Sachse's passport, etc. My father, Martin Sachse, died in 1977. There were three Sachse brothers in this country: Richard, Martin, and Gerhard.

Andy, by the way, is the one who started all this as far as I am concerned, and I am so glad he talked me into submitting a sample to 23andMe.

Laureen, if you are ever in the Sacramento area, I would love to meet you. My days in Southern California are at an end. My husband, Bert, and I lived in Los Angeles for 52 years until we moved to Elk Grove to be near our daughter, Nancy, and our son, Andy, in San Francisco. Bert died in 2004, and I live alone just 4 miles from Nancy.

I have seen on the TV that you have been flooded in the Riverside area. I do hope you had no danger.

Do keep in touch,
Love, Heide

Heide helped us both uncover our true personal histories. It's remarkable how different people can be about sharing, openness and truth. Jonathan was in awe at what was unfolding and it actually helped bring us closer. Once again, we have to thank science, along with the generous heart of another human being, for connecting us with family.

Chapter Nineteen – The Best Laid Plans

*Each friend represents a world in us, a world not born until they arrive,
and it is only by this meeting that a new world is born.*
~Anais Nin

My husband and the rest of my family, including my mother-in-law, as well as all my friends who knew what was going with this crazy journey I was on, would ask me on occasion, "Do you want to meet Jonathan?" or "When are you going to meet Jonathan?"

It seemed to me like the natural progression for this sort of thing. I felt ready. I had spent a great deal of time during my lifetime thinking about my biological family and wondering about them. I had spent many of my adult years searching – first for Margaret, and then, in a way, for Jonathan. Many times, subconsciously or consciously (probably both) I would envision a reunion of sorts and a familial relationship (or at least a friendship) that would be easy and natural, much like a relationship with an old friend. The kind of relationship where months or even years could go by without seeing one another, but upon meeting, no matter how much time had passed or how much strife, struggle, or chaos that had been separately endured, the connection would be immediate, and the separateness would be mutually understood and appreciated.

The reality of the situation was that I could be rejected

(again). I never had a reunion with Margaret, and I'm fairly certain I never will. I was hoping it would be different for me and Jonathan, although I didn't like to describe our potential meeting as a reunion. Not only had we never met, but he never knew I existed. How could it be a "reunion?" By definition, a reunion is a "reuniting of persons after separation." I liked to think of it more as a meeting of two common hearts and souls.

I had to keep reminding myself, however, that I was the one who invested the time and effort to find Jonathan. I had time to mentally prepare – I knew (more or less) what I was looking for. Jonathan, however, was simply found. No time to prepare. Not only that, the revelation that I was a long-lost daughter he never knew he had hit him hard. He didn't believe it at first. I had to convince him with the information that I had. And, of course, there was the DNA evidence.

Jonathan warmed up to the idea that I was, indeed, his daughter. That still didn't fix the fact that he doesn't remember. Perhaps the idea of meeting me (and facing a truth that he cannot even remember) represented a life-changing event that he was just not ready for. He was also preoccupied with building his own family tree (which also happens to be my family tree) and dealing with a new reality about his parents.

And, what of this newfound side of the family that even he wasn't aware of? I don't know why I felt so hesitant to claim it as my own. It felt like it was *his* family first. Once he claimed it and chewed it up a bit, maybe I'd feel like I could have a slice. I could let Jonathan feast on the bounty of new information about himself, his parents, and his family. Maybe, I shouldn't just barge in. There was a lot of information to absorb. He's a bastard child, just like me. I didn't think he saw that coming. He didn't even bear the name of his own father. I wondered how it made him feel now that he knew the information on his birth certificate was false? Why would his mother keep secrets from him all those years? Was that something he'd even want to talk about with me? If we were to meet, would I even want to talk about that? What *would* I talk to him about? *What matters?* It was all so overwhelming.

Jonathan had made a plan to come down to California for a visit to his see his old childhood sweetheart – the mysterious Marian Michaels – in December of 2014. Marian lived in Northern California, not too far from Heide, who lived near Sacramento. Jonathan and I had both communicated with Heide about the discovery of Jonathan's father's true identity and the unfolding story about that side of the family for several months. Jonathan wanted to make a side trip to visit Heide while he was there and share photos and information with her. Jonathan told me the dates he would be in California, but didn't provide any specifics about when he would make arrangements to visit with Heide. The wheels started turning in my head.

I thought it would be reasonable for me to drive up to Sacramento and meet up with them both. It was about a seven-hour drive from my home in Riverside to the Sacramento area, but I was willing to do it to meet some of my biological family. It wasn't exactly an ideal time to go, however. Christmas was coming up, and my birthday was on December 15. No real plans were being made for my birthday – the big five-oh was the year before, and I was just fine ignoring the fifty-first anniversary of my birth. We were also busy with Guy's mother, who had been ill and was just getting released from the hospital. A lot was going on, for sure, but certainly I could make some time for something this important. I invited Zach to come along so he could keep me company and help out with the drive. His reward would be a wild road trip with his mom and an opportunity to meet his grandfather and some of the biological family members he never knew he had. He reluctantly agreed to go.

Heide thought it was a great idea. In fact, she loved the idea and was excited at the opportunity to be a part of the experience of Jonathan and me meeting for the first time. But, she wasn't sure of Jonathan's itinerary – she only knew the dates he would be in California. I wrote to Jonathan in early November and asked what he thought of the idea of me driving up to meet with him and Heide. He didn't respond. I just figured he was busy with the holidays and the museum.

Days went by, then a week. I still didn't hear from him. But, I was hopeful. I made a hotel reservation based on Heide's recommendation and mapped out my drive. I made plans for Zach and me to stop along the way at Harris Ranch and a couple of wineries. Why not make an adventure of it?

I kept in touch with Heide, who confirmed that she had not heard from Jonathan, either. We were both left hanging. Waiting. My plans were tight because of the timing. If Jonathan could not arrange to get to Heide's house near Sacramento at some point during the first weekend of his visit, I would not be able to meet him. Heide, on the other hand, was hopeful he'd get in touch with her and make arrangements at some point during his two-week stay. It was unnerving. Not to mention, a rare storm was brewing in the Pacific Northwest that was set to hit just before the first weekend in December. We don't often get powerful storms here, but when we do get a big one, it can shut down the main highway connecting southern and northern California, so I was a little worried. In addition, the weather during that time had been complicated by the long-standing drought in California, coupled with the fire-ravaged hillsides, potential flooding, and mudslides. All of that, on top of not hearing from Jonathan about his plans, was stressing me out. Apparently, Heide was a little worried, too.

Laureen,

I have not heard from Jonathan about his itinerary. I do wish he'd be a bit more forthcoming with his plans.

I've thought of your driving here and have been concerned about the weather as well as your difficulties at home. I hope it will all work out for you but will certainly understand if it doesn't, as far as I am concerned. You and I will meet some day.

You don't have to respond to this right away. I just wanted to touch base with you again and let you know that I would understand if we have to put our plans on hold. I do hope your mother-in-law's health improves soon.

Love, Heide

Heide and I were on the same page.

Hi Heide!

I appreciate your concern, as I am having similar concerns of my own. Jonathan admitted to me at one point a while back that he is a bit of a hermit – doesn't do much between the museum and his art (which is a solitary endeavor). We've gone quite a long time in between correspondence at times.

In any event, I may put off the trip. I do most definitely want to meet you! And Jonathan, of course, but I don't know what to do if he doesn't respond. And I know the weather is supposed to get funky in the next few days. I was planning on bringing my 23 year old son, Zach, with me (Jonathan's grandson). Was looking forward to the trip, and a stop at Harris Ranch for lunch. In any event, I will let you know in the next day or two for sure.

I so appreciate your concern – thank you so much.

Love,
Laureen

I waited until just a few days before we were supposed to leave. Zach and I had planned on leaving Riverside on Thursday and getting up to the Sacramento area on Friday. On Wednesday, I canceled my hotel reservation and let Heide know.

Heide, of course, was understanding.

The storm came and went. There was quite a bit of rain, which was just too much for the dry California earth to handle. There was flash flooding and mudslides in the burn areas. I was worried about Jonathan, which seemed weird. Did he make it to his destination?

In addition to the weather and my canceled travel plans, a lot was going on that December. My mother-in-law had minor surgery and she was moved to a convalescent/rehab facility, where she ended up staying through the holidays. My birthday came and went without much fanfare, which was okay with me. My husband was getting ready to start a new position with his job as an attorney for the county.

I never heard from Jonathan during his trip. Neither did Heide, until she reached out to him once again. She was apparently just as frustrated as I was.

Jonathan:

Are you in California? Would be helpful to know your plans.

Thanks.
Heide

It took him two days, but he did respond.

Hi Heide:

I am indeed here but have run into a rather serious problem. While helping Marian, my old friend I have known for years, I tore a ligament in my leg. I have been laid up for four days and am now just able to walk without much pain.

I saw a doctor and he advised me to rest and keep my foot raised. This has been a disaster for me in that I had plans to visit you and another old friend in San Francisco.

Marian and I made plans that also had to be canceled and now this damn storm is roaring in. If Marian and I can get out of here I will make every effort to visit you and Andy. That was, after all, the primary reason I came down at this time.

I am sorry I didn't call you or Andy earlier

Love to you all, and I am so sorry about all this... I was so looking forward to an easy vacation with the extra joy of meeting you.

Jonathan Winter

I appreciated that Heide forwarded me her exchange with

Jonathan. She knew I was feeling deflated. His message didn't help. I shouldn't have had any expectations. I shouldn't have just assumed it would be easy. I shouldn't have encroached so boldly on his plans. And, maybe I shouldn't take apart his message, but he did say that meeting Heide and Andy was the main reason he had planned the trip. No mention of meeting his long-lost daughter. Maybe, he didn't get my messages? Perhaps, he was just avoiding meeting me. I think it was just too overwhelming for him to deal with the possibility of meeting me *and* his new cousin, Heide. Heide had been the one who had given him the key to *his* identity. That's what he was looking for all along. He was never looking for me. I was just a kind of unwanted side dish he got along with the main meal. Like the soggy green beans you get with your meatloaf.

Interestingly enough, shortly after Heide forwarded Jonathan's message to me, I received an email directly from him. He must have been feeling guilty. Maybe, he was feeling like he owed me some sort of explanation. It was weird, though, that he didn't mention my plan to travel north to visit.

Greetings, Laureen!

What a trip! I arrived here in northern California after a 5 hour stint stuck in a traffic jam on the way from Sacramento to Grass Valley. Flooding and an accident on the highway kept us at a standstill for about five hours. It was pure horror!

Then... while helping Marian move some things into her garage I somehow tore a ligament in my leg and was laid up for days with instructions from the doctor to keep my leg elevated.

Anyway, I finally called Heide and talked to her... there is a major storm here now and we are advised to keep off the roads because of flash floods... (check out the weather in Grass Valley and Sacramento.)

I am still going to try to visit Heide if possible but am already planning another visit after the new year.... I will plan enough time to visit both you and Heide, maybe three weeks or so. That would be wonderful in that I would have no obligations at the Museum and would not have that worry about that.

I do want to meet you and it would be just wonderful for us all to get together. There is so much for all of us to learn about our lives. I am now wondering more and more about my mother.

In any event, I had planned to call you when I arrived but things just didn't work out as I had hoped. I am sorry I didn't keep you informed of the situation.

I hope you and your family have a great Christmas.

Keep well and love to all there,
Jonathan

It was something. I felt strange, though. Like an afterthought. But, for some reason, I felt like I wanted to take the pressure off him. He must have been feeling like he had some obligation to me, but he didn't really want to acknowledge it. I took the reins. Maybe, that would be easier for him. Once again, eager to please.

Hi Jonathan!

I hope you made it home all in one piece. Sorry your trip to Cali didn't turn out as planned. Hope you're healing — and hope you got to enjoy some of your time with Marian.

I had planned to come up to meet with Heide (and hoped you would join us) the first weekend you were in Cali. I hadn't heard from you about your definite plans while here so I just made arrangements to get my butt up there. I realize now that was a bit presumptuous, but Heide was on board with my plans and expecting me December 6. But when we never heard from you, we decided it would probably be best for me to cancel and not make the drive up. Just as well, though, lots of family stuff going on down here — and I know the weather was treacherous everywhere that weekend. And apparently you ran into some trouble, as well, with the weather and your injury! What a disaster!

I know you mentioned you were going to try to come back down sometime in January — that would be great. Please keep me posted if you do. I would so love to meet Heide — what a generous soul! But I would also like to get some feedback from you about what you think of me coming up to Bellingham. I do not want to disrupt anything you've got going on – but I would love to come up and see the museum and anything else you'd like to show me. I don't want to let this go – I do want to meet you and I think it would be good for me to make the journey. I will arrange for a hotel and work around your schedule to spend as much or as little time with you as you can allow. No pressure. I don't know about January – I think the weather scares me most of all (I'm a real Southern California girl!) – I can handle cold, but probably not a bunch of snow! Anyway, let me know what you think about when it would be convenient for you, or give me your thoughts in general if you are even wary of the situation or the prospect of meeting me, I totally understand. I want it to be easy – and I promise it will.

With everything going on around here I haven't had much time to get back to the research about our family. I do want to find out more about your mom (my grandmother).

Again, I hope you're healing and getting ready for the Holidays! Hope to hear from you soon.

Love,
Laureen

And then… crickets. I received a short message from him on Christmas Eve:

After returning from my visit south I have been somewhat in the doldrums… I had a wonderful time visiting Marian, but between the weather and my leg…. well I didn't get to visit with Heide nor with you. I was looking forward to talking with Heide. I still have so many questions.

Well, the new year will provide a new opportunity to visit and I am making that a top priority for this new year.

Forgive the overall lack of communication.

I hope you have a great Christmas.

ENJOY!
Jonathan

Still no comment about the possibility of me heading up north. I got it. He was having a bout of the doldrums. I received a couple more emails from him over the next few weeks, but no acknowledgment of my offer to travel north to Washington. No talk of returning to California, either. Now, I was in the doldrums.

About this time, I was contacted by a casting producer who was putting together a proposal for a television series for a major international cable network. The idea for the show was to highlight different scenarios and situations involving people who had been separated from a family member at birth. She wasn't just interested in adoption stories. She was looking for interesting stories and dramatic tales of kidnapping, babies switched in the hospital, twins separated as infants and reunited later in life, etc. She explained the tone of the show was to be uplifting; she wanted to tell individual stories and showcase searches and reunions.

The woman who contacted me had read my blog and was intrigued by the interesting twists and turns in my story over the years. She knew about the discovery of my bio mom years ago and understood there would be no reunion on that end of the story. She wanted to know if I had met Jonathan yet.

"No. We actually had plans to meet in December around the time of my birthday, but that plan fell through for a number of reasons," I told her.

What I really wanted to tell her was that he flaked on me and that I was beginning to think there would never be a meeting. I was already anticipating her next question.

"Do you think Jonathan would be agreeable to us filming your reunion if we helped to arrange it for the show?"

I knew the answer to that question, but I was stalling. It would be exciting to finally meet Jonathan – whether on camera or not. I started having visions of me and Jonathan hugging and skipping hand in hand through his museum (I assumed my biological father could skip like I could). Then, I pictured his art – all sparkly – I saw a handmade 14-karat gold mask in my likeness. It was so beautiful! He made it just for me and the reunion and the show!

But, that wasn't Jonathan. That wasn't reality. Just another adoptee fantasy. I knew in my heart that an on-camera reunion would be too much for him. He'd barely gotten his head around the fact that he has a middle-aged daughter he never knew about. He was just figuring out who his own parents were. He was an old hippie. In his own words, he was a hermit. A reunion on camera would most likely be out of the question. And, he hadn't even addressed my inquiries about coming up to Washington – how would I bring up an on-camera reunion?

So, I didn't. But, I did write and ask more of a direct question about meeting. I figured it was time to get down to business. Did he want to meet me or not? Let's quit avoiding the big adopted elephant in the room.

Hi Jonathan,

I am sorry I have not been in touch in the last few weeks. I've been a little disconnected, I guess. I've also been a little troubled by your lack of response to my request to meet and my offer to come up to Bellingham. But really, I do understand your trepidation and your concerns. And I know you are just discovering a world of new information about our family through Heide and it must be overwhelming. I cannot imagine at age 70 discovering that you have a 50 year old daughter! And then, discovering your father's true identity just months later! It's your journey, as well, and I understand.

I do hope we can stay in touch, as I love hearing about your art, the museum and whatever information you share with me about your life and your family. I would love to see your "world" up in Bellingham if the time is right for you sometime in the future.

My life is an open book – I don't have anything to hide. I apologize if you've ever felt threatened by my assertions or intrusions. I just want to know everything I can – to fill my soul and my heart with everything I can that is real and right. I know sometimes what is real and right for me may not be real and right for everyone else.

As for the rest of the family, Garrett finished his first semester of high school with straight A's! He also was awarded Junior Varsity MVP by his football coaches! We're so proud. He's just started baseball season now. Games haven't started yet, but we're looking forward to it. I've attached a picture of Garrett I took with his football coach when he was awarded the MVP award.

Zach is still here at home, looking for work, planning to move back out, but having difficulty finding work in his music. He is also quite a good golfer and has been spending a lot of his spare time golfing – nearly every day. He's thinking of looking into work that is somehow related to golf – perhaps as an assistant pro or teaching. I'm glad I'm not in my twenties just starting out. The world has changed so much!

Guy started his new job with the County Counsel after being a prosecutor for over 25 years. I think the idea of change was difficult for him, but he's doing well.

Hope to hear from you soon.

Love,
Laureen

He responded to this email and told me he hadn't seen my previous emails expressing my desire to come to Washington. I resent them immediately. He read them. Then, this:

Laureen,

I have looked through all my mail both the Museum account and this one. I never received these emails. I think I mentioned we were having problems with email some time ago and we installed a new spam filter. I just don't know why I would not have received your mail.

Please know that I would enjoy meeting you. My feelings about you are very difficult for me to put into words. There is little doubt now in my mind that you are my daughter. My confusion comes from the lack of connection with your mom and the fact that so many years have gone by without any knowledge of your existence. But please understand that I am open to knowing you and your family and you should know there is nothing negative here.

Like you, I am pretty much an open book. As time passes and the years accumulate, I find myself looking at the world much differently than I did when I was younger. I guess most people change as they get older. As I have mentioned before, I am a bit of a hermit. I know it is limiting to me in many things I want to do, but I have been like this for too long to change and I think it may actually feed my creativity. Who the hell knows!

Before you come please give me at least at least a week's notice so I can make sure I don't have some major event going on. We have been scheduling science events at various schools around town and they can often take a good part of the day. Our educational director plans these things and I tag along to demonstrate the scientific side. I enjoy showing youngsters this history.

I am working more and more on my art, although these revelations about my family have changed the way I see things. It is hard to put my finger on just how it affects my work but it does.

It will indeed be good to share some time together and get more at ease. Let me know what you may plan and I will try to make your visit a good one.

Write back and let me know what you are thinking.

Love to you,
Jonathan

Jonathan even sent me some photos in another email soon after. The photos melted my heart: his cat, Mitch; some photos of his recent artwork; a picture of his tiny abode. He also included a photo of Megan, his daughter, and his granddaughter, Leona. It was still hard for me to wrap my head around the fact that I had a sister. It was strange; I still felt like I had to have someone's permission before I could claim a person as a relative. Is that another weird adoption thing? I kept referring to Jonathan's parents as *his* father, and *his* mother, rather than *my* grandfather and grandmother. I knew in my heart I had just as much of a *right* to claim them as my own relatives by blood as he did. Of course, I also knew no one really has a right or a claim to another human being. That sounds absurd. I didn't want to claim anyone. I just wanted to meet them.

Chapter Twenty – Anticipation

Nothing ever becomes real 'til it is experienced.
~John Keats

I chose Easter weekend. Even though Guy and I usually acknowledged the holiday with a feast and gathering of friends, our immediate family stopped celebrating Easter once my boys were too old for Easter egg hunts and the Easter Bunny. We didn't attend church regularly as a family, so Easter weekend, with Good Friday kicking it off, seemed like a good time to travel. It was the start of Garrett's spring break week, so I could return on Monday and still be home for most of his time off. It was in the middle of baseball season, but he wouldn't have any baseball games over the holiday weekend, so I wouldn't miss anything. I shared my idea with Jonathan. He checked with Megan and the rest of the family and agreed it was a good time for me to come up.

I was hoping once the plans were in place I might hear from Megan, Jonathan's daughter. I was looking forward to meeting my sister. Although I didn't hear from Megan directly, Jonathan assured me everyone was okay with my visit. Not only was Megan "okay" with me visiting, I received an invitation to stay at her home. Jonathan emailed me:

I spoke to Megan about your possible visit and she offered a spare bedroom. I live in the adjacent garage which has been converted to a small apartment. I like it... less clutter although I seem to endlessly add

things... it is the collector in me, no doubt.
   Keep well, and my best to you and your family,

   Love,
   Jonathan

That was a generous offer, but I was worried about invading their space. I knew this whole thing was really turning Jonathan's life upside down, and I figured part of Megan's trepidation about communicating with me had something to do with being protective of her father. I explained to Jonathan that I thought everyone would be more comfortable if I just stayed in a hotel close by. I wanted our meeting and visit to be easy. I also thought it would be a good idea for me to have a refuge to escape to, if needed. Not that I expected anything bad to happen, but I had no idea what to expect emotionally. And, what if they didn't like me? What if I didn't like them? What if it was just plain awkward? As it turns out, he was a little nervous, too.

   Laureen,

   I am a little worried that I will not meet your expectations... I know that must sound odd, but I know I am a bit of an eccentric in that I am not a very sociable person. I rarely go out and don't generally enjoy crowds. I am, however, looking forward to spending time learning about you and sharing my life with you. I have pulled out all the photo albums we have and I am sure you will enjoy looking at them. It will be great just talking.
   I am especially interested in what you have discovered about my mother... I just have so many questions.
   Anyway, I am glad you are coming. I'm looking forward to showing you the museum and giving you a private tour! Be sure to bring your camera...... there is nothing like seeing 5,000,000,000 volts of electricity... lightning... few ever get to see this flow of electrons... usually we see such things as a flash. Here, the flash lasts for 15 to 20 seconds. It is beautiful.
   I find myself now slowly pulling away from the Museum in order to

spend more time on my art. I am lucky to have my shop here at home.

I have no idea what your vision is of me. As I said before, I am essentially an old hippie. After discovering the information about my father and mother and gaining an understanding of how and why I was able to do the things I have done in my life, I feel almost reborn. The understanding has been transforming in a way that is difficult to explain. I will share those thoughts with you when I see you.

Love to you, kiddo,
Jonathan

Chapter Twenty-One –The Fog Lifts

Clarity and consistency are not enough;
the quest for truth requires humility and effort.
~Tariq Ramadan

I decided to travel solo. I was looking forward to being on my own for this trip. My husband and my boys were supportive of my personal journey, and Guy did offer to go with me, but I knew if he were with me, I would be distracted by constantly keeping tabs on how he was doing during the trip. Would he be bored, or was there something he'd rather do or see instead of tagging along with me for the entire weekend? I also thought it would be important to have this experience on my own so I wouldn't be tempted, either consciously or subconsciously, to gauge my emotions based on what I thought Guy was thinking, or to play up or down my emotions or reactions for any reason. I didn't want to feel like I was measuring my reactions or being careful with my words. I wanted to experience everything authentically and honestly.

My schedule for the week leading up to the trip was jampacked with all kinds of family business. In addition to school, Garrett had two baseball games and a chiropractor appointment, as well as baseball practice on the nights that there weren't any games. I had a dentist appointment on Tuesday. There was a mandatory meeting at school on

Thursday evening after the baseball game for parents of football players to plan for next season. I had also set aside a day to take my mother-in-law out for shopping and lunch. There wasn't much time to think about or to prepare mentally for my adventure – which I think was probably a good thing. The week zoomed by.

Once on the plane, I closed my eyes and took a deep breath. I exhaled slowly. It felt as though I had been holding my breath for days. I let the reality of the situation wash over me like a huge wave. I wasn't scared or nervous. I was feeling more relaxed than I had felt in months.

I thought about the future and what meeting Jonathan and his family would be like. Would it be easy? Would meting these people make me a different person? Did adoption make me feel a certain way?

Everything I had been told or taught to believe as a child about my adoption was that it was good, simple, and straightforward. *Be grateful. You were chosen. You are lucky.*

I *was* grateful. My life as an adoptee most definitely didn't suck, but what was missing was an acknowledgment that being adopted naturally comes with questions, emotions, and even fears. Being adopted also comes with confines and rules that have been imposed not only by those individuals closest to me (like parents who never openly discussed adoption), but also by the law and by strangers who can't even begin to understand, despite their sincere efforts to make sense of the enigma of adoption on my behalf. The mantra had always been: *Don't question who you are, how you fit in, or where you came from. Just be the person "they" want you to be. You have no right to self-discovery.*

But, now it seemed that the adoption fog was finally lifting. What was in front of me was real. *Real* history and truth. And, Jonathan – he found his real name, too. His real self. Our lives were changed forever.

I thought about Margaret. She preferred that I stay out of her life completely. I was to remain invisible as far as she was concerned. For so long, Margaret's rejection defined me when it came to thinking about my adoption. It took me some time and soul searching to realize that my existence and the truth about it mattered, even if Margaret felt otherwise. I finally turned the rejection into a *redirection*. I accepted that Margaret will never know me. And, I didn't need to know her.

The anger and the pain of the rejections were melting away. I know now that the rejection had to be realized and experienced before any redirection or new path would take hold. If you would have asked me twenty years ago if I was angry about Margaret's second rejection of me, I would have told you flat out, "*No.*" But, in reality, I was denying it. I pushed the anger and the confusion deep down. Now, I was finally finding answers about who I really was. I could accept that I might never know my story in its entirety – that there might still be gaps and questions in the grand scheme of it all. It was okay.

Chapter Twenty-Two – He's No Troglodyte

So many people are shut up tight inside themselves like boxes,
yet they would open up, unfolding quite wonderfully,
if only you were interested in them.
~Sylvia Plath

Seattle was gray and drizzly when the plane touched down late in the morning. The dank and dreary weather didn't match my buoyant mood. I was determined to not allow the weather to bring me down. Once off the plane, I set off to pick up my rental car. I still had a two-hour drive to Bellingham.

My phone rang while I was at the rental car counter. I fumbled around in my purse to find it, but didn't get to it in time. I finished all the initialing and signing and put my driver's license and credit card back in my wallet. With car keys in hand, I dragged my suitcase and other belongings away from the counter so I could dig around for my phone. One missed call. It was Jonathan.

I put down my bags and focused my attention on the phone as I pushed the button to call him back. I don't know why a feeling of dread washed over me at that very moment. Maybe it was the weather. Maybe I was just used to being disappointed. That feeling dissolved as soon as he answered the phone.

"Hello, kiddo!" He had started calling me "kiddo" in

emails and during the few telephone and Skype conversations we had had over the last few months. It was endearing, and I liked it. I wondered if he called Megan "kiddo," too, or if it was a term he had assigned to me.

"Hi! Sorry I couldn't get to the phone, I was at the rental car counter. I'm here, and I'm excited to get on the road to Bellingham! I figure I've got about a two-hour drive?"

"Yes, that sounds about right… that is, if the weather and traffic cooperate. Give me a ring when you get to the hotel."

Wow. This was really happening. I was going to meet my biological father. And, he actually sounded like he was looking forward to meeting me.

I drove north out of Seattle. How different it was from California. Through Everett, Marysville, and on up through Mt. Vernon, the scenery just kept getting more beautiful. Views of the ocean gave way to stretches of open farmland and rolling mountains with cascading forests and trees so dense I couldn't see past the first few rows. I wanted to pull over to take some pictures, but it was still drizzling, and I wasn't familiar with the area, so I just kept driving. As I was rolling along, I spotted a waterfall on the steep mountainside to my right not too far from the highway. I had never seen such a thing! I had seen waterfalls before, but this was unusual – just hanging, like a 3-D mural right there on the side of the highway.

I thought of the time several years ago when I had been visiting my son, Zach, who was living in Mammoth, California. It was a beautiful day, and Zach and I decided to make the day-long hike up to Rainbow Falls. Once we found the grand waterfall, we were rewarded with its splendor and majesty as we looked on in reverence. It was amazing. But, seeing this rogue waterfall there on the side of the highway in Washington was something else entirely. I thought about the locals who drove by all day long, just matter-of-factly glancing at the waterfall's wondrous beauty as they went about their commute or errands. The simplicity of it struck me as almost absurd. I wondered if the other drivers even noticed it.

I found the hotel – thanks to the GPS on my phone – and

unloaded my stuff. I felt strange checking in by myself. I couldn't remember the last time I had been to a hotel or traveled alone. I spent some time unpacking and organizing things in my room. I was only going to be there for three nights, but I wanted everything to be just right.

Once settled in, I called Jonathan. He had been waiting for my call. He insisted that he come right over so we could meet, talk, and maybe go grab something to eat. I could have just as easily driven to his house to meet him, but I figured the hotel was probably a better venue for our first meeting. After all, I was sure it crossed his mind (more than once?) that I might be some kind of nut. And hell, I didn't really know him, either. Better safe than sorry.

I hung up the phone and stood in the middle of my hotel room.

Now what?

I looked nervously around. Everything was unpacked and in its place. I walked over to the full-length mirror. Should I change my clothes? Fix my hair? Touch up my make-up? Did any of that matter?

I sat down at the desk and turned on my laptop. I connected to the hotel Wi-Fi while I waited. I checked in on Facebook. There were a few well-wishes on my page from friends who knew I was on my way to meeting Jonathan. On my Newsfeed, recipes for deviled eggs, baked ham, and spring vegetables were being shared. I had almost forgotten that Easter was just two days away.

There was a knock on the door. My heart jumped, and my whole body suddenly felt strange… like I was not in control of my own movements. Somehow, I got up out of the chair and walked to the door. I swear, I felt like I was floating. *Here goes nothing.* I swung the door open. There stood Jonathan. *My father.*

He looked just like his pictures, complete with his wool vest, silver ponytail, and his signature leather hat. In his left hand, he held a single red rose. Without hesitation, he held out the rose and said, "Welcome."

I took the rose, and he stepped forward. We hugged. I'm

sure it was me that pulled away first, but I just had to look at him again. I could have just stood there in the doorway and stared at him for hours, but that would have been weird, so I invited him in.

We sat next to each other on the edge of the bed and made small talk about my drive from Seattle and the weather. I told him I was fascinated by the beauty of the landscape and about the waterfall I saw off the highway.

"I think I know right where that is," he offered.

When I came home from my trip a few days later, a friend asked me about the moment Jonathan and I met. He asked if there were tears, or if I was overcome by any kind of primal emotion. There weren't, and I wasn't. It just felt natural. Real and right. Conversation was easy and without pretense or agenda. There was an instantaneous familiarity and generosity between us. It was something unique; something I never had experienced before. It was the first time I had been treated as family without feeling like I had to earn it first. I enjoyed this notion of family, and I felt incredibly special at that moment.

We left the hotel to grab a bite to eat. Jonathan took me to a little Mexican restaurant – nothing fancy – and we ordered at the counter. We found a table and continued the conversation, making plans for the rest of the weekend. It was surreal sitting across from him – I could stare all I wanted. I wanted to remember everything about him. It seemed so odd – this total stranger sitting across from me was my *father*.

Back at the hotel after dinner, Jonathan walked with me back up to my room. When we got inside, he surprised me when he went straight for a book that had been sitting on the bed. He said he noticed it when he first came in and wanted to take a look at it. It was *Mountain Drive, Santa Barbara's Pioneer Bohemian Community* by Elias Chiacos. The book tells the enchanting true story of the infamous hippies and artists who lived in the hills above Santa Barbara in the 1950s and 60s, with lots of great black and white photos of the characters and the debauchery that defined the Bohemian community. Jonathan was part of this community in spirit. He didn't live there – he was only in his teens during the community's heyday, and he had a well-appointed home near Franceschi Park where he lived with his mother. But, he knew all about the unconventional lifestyles and the wild parties up along the Drive. He knew many of the infamous players, including its founder, Bobby Hyde, who lived in the Bohemian commune. I gave him the book to take home and read. He was delighted. We hugged and said goodnight.

After Jonathan left, I got ready for bed. The red rose was still lying on the nightstand. Before crawling into bed, I grabbed a plastic cup from the tray in the bathroom and filled it with water for the rose. Even without a proper vase, the rose looked beautiful. It was not fully bloomed yet, but the petals were just starting to unfold to reveal a perfect burst of complicated beauty. As I drifted off to sleep, I was thinking about how the rose symbolized a whole new dimension to my identity. I thought after becoming a parent there would be no more new dimensions. I was wrong.

At the farmers' market the next day, Jonathan and I chose some fresh field greens and a locally made blueberry sauce to pair with some salmon that he had at home for dinner. I was looking forward to cooking with him and meeting my sister later in the day. The market was huge and colorful and included local crafters and artists hawking their wares in addition to the local organic produce and locally made food items. We took some time to walk through the crafts and artists and came across several jewelry makers. I checked out some of the handmade jewelry, but really, I was watching Jonathan. He walked right past most of the vendors without a second glance, but he would stop when he spotted an artist who displayed jewelry or metalwork that interested him. I loved watching him engage and talk shop with the other artists and jewelry makers.

The next stop was the local bead shop in downtown Bellingham that displayed and sold some of Jonathan's work.

This was no ordinary bead store. Karen, the barefooted owner, was an enthusiastic collector of antique beads and other unique embellishments, as well as vintage textiles and unusual artifacts from all over the world. Jonathan introduced me to Karen as simply, *Laureen*. Karen smiled and nodded and told me she was happy to finally meet me. I got the impression that Jonathan had told her our story. She led me to the large glass cabinet in the middle of the store that held a selection of Jonathan's jewelry and other pieces. I asked if she would unlock the cabinet so I could touch and hold some of the pieces. She did. There were handmade silver and gold lockets, intricate figurines, chains, rings, and other jewelry with precious and semi-precious stones, along with reproductions of small Native American tribal ceremonial bowls and masks. Some of the items were primitive-looking, reflecting the influence from the Chumash, the Native American people who lived in and around Santa Barbara where Jonathan grew up and where he first spread his artistic wings. Jonathan told me the stories behind the some of the pieces. One of the masks on the wall even had real human teeth.

Jonathan also told me he'd been thinking about making a piece for me. Something that would represent our history and our relationship. He designed each piece he made, whether it was a piece of jewelry, a mask, or something else, by sketching it out first, so it would be a while before I would see what our relationship looked like as interpreted by Jonathan. I was touched that our budding relationship was a source of creative inspiration for him.

After the bead shop, we headed to the museum. I was excited to finally get to see the place that was built from the ground up by Jonathan and his business partner. I was treated to a VIP tour with Jonathan as my personal guide. We strolled through the museum while he explained the significance of the items I showed interest in. The collections included rare items used in scientific electrical experiments dating from the 1600s through the 1940s and the Golden Age of Radio.

The radios were Jonathan's specialty. There were

thousands of radios in the collection, many from his own personal collection. There were also rare music boxes, early phonographs, and many examples of early communication and radio broadcasting technology and memorabilia. The museum even housed and ran its own radio station, which focused on showcasing the museum's massive media collection. The station was also in the process of developing and cultivating local programming that would provide educational, cultural, and historical value to residents of the community.

Jonathan's knowledge about the evolution of the technology blew me away. He was articulate, patient, and thoughtful as he answered my questions about some of the items.

My favorite moment was when he demonstrated the antique American-made Criterion Music Box for me. I had never seen a music box like this before. The case was made of oak, hand-carved like a beautiful piece of furniture, with a metal hand crank on one side. The hinged top opened like an old record player to reveal a mechanism holding a large metal disc. Once cranked, the hidden spring motor went to work, slowly spinning the metal disc, which was driven by a gear that caught perforations around the edge of the disc. A comb – a long metal piece with finely tuned tines – was situated parallel to the disc, with the tines of the comb perpendicular to the disc. The disc was studded with tiny pins at the correct spacing to produce music by displacing the teeth of the comb at the correct time. The tines of the comb "ring," or sound, as they slip off the pins.

Jonathan explained that this particular beautifully-crafted, hand-cranked music box was made in the late 1800s and had belonged to his mother, Millie (my grandmother!). He told me how he remembered his mother playing it in their living room when he was young. As a child, he was not allowed to touch it.

Jonathan cranked up the music box. The sound was bright and full. The music was sweet. I got goosebumps as I listened to the tinny melody.

When we finished the tour, Jonathan led me into a small

auditorium where the MegaZapper Electrical Show was performed every weekend. There was no show that day because it was Easter Weekend, but, luckily for me, one of Jonathan's colleagues was there doing some work on the giant MegaZapper when we went in. The MegaZapper was a huge, nine-foot-tall Tesla Coil (one of the largest in the country) that produces titan-sized lightning bolts right before the eyes of astonished museum guests. Jonathan and I sat in the front row of the empty auditorium. After a couple of assurances about safety and warnings about the noise, I was treated to a personal display of stunning (and loud!), ten-foot arcs of purple lightning. It was incredible to see so close! There was even a "lightning cage" in the corner of the showroom. Jonathan explained that a volunteer from the audience can sit inside the specially built metal cage-like enclosure and be bombarded with four million volts of electricity. It's perfectly safe, I'm told!

Before we left the museum, I was introduced to some of Jonathan's colleagues and others who work at the museum. It was clear that he is regarded as the patriarch of the museum and is very much respected. I was so proud. Jonathan picked up a couple of books that were for sale behind the counter and handed them to me as gifts. *Where Discovery Sparks Imagination, A Pictorial History of Radio and Electricity* was written by John Jenkins, the former Microsoft executive and Jonathan's partner and fellow curator at the museum. *Radiola, The Golden Age of RCA* was written by Eric P. Wenaas, a fellow collector and expert on everything radio and wireless. I enjoyed looking through Jenkins' book (there were lots of pictures of the things I had seen at the museum), but I have to admit, while Wenaas' book gave me some understanding and appreciation for how damned smart Jonathan is. Most of the information was way over my non-scientific head.

Finally, it was time to go to Jonathan's home and meet the rest of the family. By this time, I felt comfortable with Jonathan, but there was something still missing. I wanted to *belong*. I wanted to connect and feel connected in that mysterious way that only blood relatives must feel. I was nervous. How would Megan react to me?

Again, Jonathan assured me that everyone was *more than okay* with the whole situation. Like *more than okay* was supposed to be reassuring. Megan had never reached out to me in the year that Jonathan and I had been in touch. I understood in the beginning that she was simply protective of her father and the rest of her family. I didn't blame her for that. She didn't know who the hell I was, claiming to be some long-lost sister she never knew about. It sounded like a dumb made-for-TV movie, or worse, some sort of scam. She probably didn't believe the seemingly convoluted story I told. Hell, Jonathan didn't believe it, either... at first.

As we drove from the museum to Jonathan's house, Bellingham's small-town vibe gave way to more rural scenery. The neighborhood where Jonathan lived was on a hill amongst a forest of trees. The neighbors were close by, but the abundance of flora surrounding the area gave the homes the feeling of being more secluded than they really were.

Jonathan's home was one of the older homes on the block. It was built in 1906. Jonathan told me the story of his home. He had purchased the house with his wife, Judith, in 1986. Most of the houses on the same street were on smaller lots and were much newer. Jonathan explained that the area surrounding his home was more rural when he moved in with his young family. Over the years, he watched the development of his neighborhood and worried that the beautiful landscape surrounding his home would be taken over by suburban sprawl.

Concerned about the future, Jonathan took it upon himself to research the building plans for the property immediately surrounding his home. Jonathan discovered the property behind his home was being divided into parcels in preparation for development. His beautiful old home was already flanked by new homes on either side and more construction was going on across the street. Development of any kind on the narrow strip between Jonathan's property and the hillside behind his home would have not only spoiled the view of the forest from his grand backyard, it would have ruined the spirit of the home. Jonathan solved the problem – he purchased the property behind his home. No one would be able to build behind his home. Jonathan did what he could to preserve his little slice of heaven.

We pulled into the gravel driveway, which was in front of a small building – I presumed the garage. Jonathan took a moment before we got out to explain.

"I own the home and the property in back, woods and all. This is where I live now." Jonathan gestured toward the tiny wooden building in front of us.

"I think I told you that Megan, Phil, and my granddaughter live in the main house now. They need more room than I do. I use the big kitchen often and we sometimes eat all together. We just come and go as we please." Jonathan hesitated, then continued.

"I'd say Phil is Megan's common-law husband. They've been together since before Leona was born. They've just never felt the need to get married. I wasn't too sure about Phil in the beginning – all the tattoos – he just seemed a little rough around the edges. But, he treats Megan and Leona just fine, and I've come to see him as family."

I didn't tell Jonathan that I had two tattoos.

Jonathan stepped out of the car and onto the crunchy gravel. I followed. I felt like a little kid. I don't know why.

He strode up the front walk and tentatively climbed the front steps. I got the feeling he didn't usually enter the home through the front door like this. From where we had parked, I could see a side door, and I'm sure there was a back door… the doors of familiarity.

We entered the house and Jonathan called out for Megan. She came into the living room holding little seven-year-old Leona's hand. Phil followed close behind. Megan and I hugged awkwardly and exchanged small gifts – I had brought her some of my blended spices and a cookbook. She gave me a beautiful scarf. There was also a note from Megan:

Laureen –

How brave of you to make this trip. I'll admit I've been a bit hesitant to embrace this experience, but as the day drew near I've grown excited. I admire your courage and look forward to getting to know you.

Love, Megan

Leona also had a gift for me. She had colored a simple picture of a few flowers and a bright, yellow sun. Scrawled across the picture in crayon in her own handwriting was a message:

I am happy to meat you.

Leona

My heart felt so full, I thought it would burst right then and there. I was so relieved and happy to be welcomed into their home. The nervousness was gone. Megan and I hugged again. This time, the hug felt real. I'm sure there was small talk after that, but I don't remember. I was just so happy to be there.

After a few minutes, Jonathan led me into the kitchen. I set the greens and the blueberry sauce on the counter. We had a little bit of time before we needed to start dinner, so Jonathan poured Megan and me a glass of wine and popped open a beer for himself. We sat down at the kitchen island and talked. After some idle chit chat and getting to know Megan a little (she was a paralegal, just like me!), I pulled out the notebook. I knew Jonathan was anxiously awaiting the debut of the *notebook*.

Chapter Twenty-Three – It's All in The Details

People are trapped in history and history is trapped in them.
~James A. Baldwin

The notebook, along with most of its contents, was a gift from one of my dearest friends, Ann. Ann is a real whiz when it comes to research. More specifically, genealogical research. That complicated stuff that makes up family trees. The same stuff that adoptees aren't generally entitled to.

Through all the years of wondering about and searching for my biological family, I had never really thought about the possibility of putting together a family tree. I just wanted some answers to some basic questions. I assumed there were *simple* answers, but boy, was I wrong about that.

Over the course of my journey and search, I had been sharing the bits and pieces of my story with my friend. Ann was fascinated by the twists and turns within the story and was eager to help me find answers that would make sense and fill in the blanks. After my needle-in-a-haystack match with Jonathan on *23andMe* and hearing Jonathan's story about not knowing *his* father, Ann took the bull by the horns and started sleuthing on her own (with my blessing, of course). She's naturally curious. And, luckily for me, she has a generous heart and a knack for helping people.

Ann had researched and put together her own extensive

Italian family tree a year earlier. She was able to piece together a family history that went back generations. Using resources on the Internet, Ann was able to pinpoint important time and place markers for significant events in her family's timeline, including the confirmation of Mafia connections! She didn't turn up any shocking surprises or reveal any long-hidden secrets, but the research she completed was interesting and invaluable to her family and she enjoyed putting it all together.

Through Ann, I discovered how remarkable the Internet and research sites like Ancestry.com are for genealogical research. Ancestry.com includes the world's largest subscription collection of genealogy databases. Subscribers can access US census records dating from 1790 through 1940, along with many Canadian, English, and Welsh records and data. There are military records, including databases of soldiers from the Revolutionary War, Civil War, and both world wars. Vital records cover many US states, Canada and the United Kingdom, and immigration records range from passenger lists for most American ports to border-crossing records. The information is mind-boggling when you think of it. A good amount of it is uploaded by other subscribers – people curious about the past and their family histories. Genealogy is indeed big business. And, Ann made my genealogy *her* business.

Ann enthusiastically researched and explored the records and data on Ancestry.com to find details about Jonathan and his mother and father. We spent several evenings together, sometimes over wine and pasta, comparing notes and putting together timelines to make sense of the bits and pieces of information we were able to find. We spent hours sitting with our heads together, staring at the computer screen searching and poring over seemingly endless amounts of data, tossing out information that obviously didn't apply (Me: *That's not him – it's the wrong birth date*) and screaming at each other when we found relevant pieces to the puzzle (Ann: *Oh. My. God! I know the neighborhood where Jonathan's father's apartment was in San Francisco!*) Ann was also from the Bay Area. Once, Ann found a particular tidbit of information that got her so riled up and excited that she screamed and nearly pushed me off my chair. We laughed. We were both excited about the possibilities.

Because we now had Jonathan's father's *real* name (from his newfound cousin, Heide), we were able to find information about him fairly easily. My paternal grandfather, Richard Sachse, was born in 1881 in Saxony, Germany. He was educated at the Dresden University of Technology, earning a degree in civil engineering. He then earned a Master of Science degree in structural engineering at the University of Hannover in Hannover, Germany.

After his education, Richard was continuously engaged in engineering work in Germany, Africa, Belgium, Norway, and the United States. In 1905, at age twenty-five, Richard came to America for good. He eventually made his way to California and married. He and his wife, Katherine, first settled in San Francisco, where Richard worked as a draftsman for the Western Pacific Railroad.

Richard and his wife had two children: a girl, Mary Elizabeth, and a boy, Franz Robert. He and his family eventually settled in a rural farming area near San Diego. Katherine and the children stayed in their sprawling ranch home in Fallbrook, but Richard kept other residences over the years in different parts of the state in order to accommodate the travel required for his demanding career. He also traveled often to Washington, D.C. in connection with his work.

In the early 1940s, Richard held the position of Director of the State Department of Natural Resources. In 1943, Richard was named California Railroad Commissioner. He traveled extensively, in demand for his expertise in everything that had anything to do with engineering, transportation, urban planning, and natural resources. Richard did consulting work for private industries, including the Southern Pacific Railroad, the Santa Fe Railway, the Western Pacific Railroad, the Los Angeles Railway, Key System of San Francisco (the local streetcar and bus lines in the East Bay, and commuter rail and bus lines connecting the East Bay to San Francisco by a ferry pier on San Francisco Bay), and the Golden Gate Bridge.

Jonathan, at age seventy when I found him, had already spent many years searching for information about his father, to no avail. He didn't even have his own father's *real name*. Why was his mother so secretive about his father? The simple answer could be, of course, *because of the affair*. But, was there more to it?

One of the few pieces of information Millie had shared with Jonathan about his father was that he had been an engineer and had worked on the Golden Gate Bridge. After Millie died, Jonathan went to work. He contacted several engineering companies in the Bay Area that he thought might have records relating to the work his father did. He also turned to the Internet and posted in several genealogical groups. In 1994, he posted in a forum on one group:

> *I am looking for any information on my father, Carl Robert Winter. I believe he was from San Francisco, born in 1899, or thereabouts. He worked for Bechtal Corp. Married to Millie Sanders of Oakland. I have not been able to turn up anything on my own. Any help appreciated. J. Winter*

He got no responses. No one could help him. That's because the information he had was all wrong. His father wasn't born in San Francisco, and he wasn't employed by Bechtal Corp. And, his name was not Carl Robert Winter.

In the kitchen, the wine and beer were loosening things up. Megan had pulled out some old photo albums, and together, we looked through some of the photos, including photos of Richard and Millie and childhood photos of Jonathan. Then, we thumbed through an album that included more recent pictures of Jonathan and his wife, Judith (Megan's mother), and Megan at various stages growing up. I enjoyed looking at these old photos. I was able to see Jonathan as a whole person, with his own real history, rather than just this guy who happened to make a baby with Margaret.

I could tell Jonathan was eager to look at the notebook. We set the old photo albums aside and started thumbing through the notebook. Some of the items needed explanation, so we turned the pages together while Megan started on dinner.

The notebook held all the information Ann and I had gathered about Millie and Richard through all our research. Of course, Jonathan knew his own mother, but he admittedly knew very little about her life prior to her becoming a mother. She was a private person. Or, was she hiding something?

We know Richard had a residence in San Francisco and was in the Bay Area often – staying for extended periods of time in an apartment he rented near Coit Tower. The information we were able to dig up on Richard and Millie confirmed that Richard was still married to his first wife, Katherine, when Jonathan was conceived, which would have been in mid-1942. *Scandalous!*

There wasn't just factual data in the notebook. Ann had even used addresses she found in the old census reports and city registries to pull up photos of the houses where Richard and his family lived at different times during their lives, including the old addresses in Germany.

Technology has made the world smaller and so much more accessible. There was so much to take in and all of it new for Jonathan. The timeline and family tree, copies of ship manifests from the turn of the nineteenth century, military draft registration cards (from both World Wars), petitions for naturalization, newspaper articles, marriage indexes, birth records, and census documents were bringing our personal and familial history to life.

There was one newspaper article that caught Jonathan's attention. Apparently, his father, Richard, had *three* children with his first wife, Katherine, not just two. From the San Francisco Chronicle:

Berkeley Boy Drowns in Ditch at Sisson
SISSON, July 3, 1919. Falling into a water wheel, in a ditch at

the Chico State Normal Winter School tent city here, Richard Sachse, Jr., 7 years old, son of Mr. and Mrs. Richard Sachse of Berkeley, was drowned before aid could reach him. Attempts at resuscitation failed. The boy's father is chief engineer of the State Railroad Commission.

I tried to read the expression on Jonathan's face. It looked like a mix of confusion, enlightenment, and astonishment. As he studied the pages of information and photos, he kept telling me how amazing it all was and how much it meant to him to have this new information. He said he felt like a different person. He grew up an only child, without his father, and without any knowledge of his prodigious family history. There were three half-siblings! All were deceased now, but to know there existed in this world relations who shared blood and ancestry – along with a rich family history – was a revelation. As I sat there watching him take in this experience of getting to know himself all over again, I knew exactly how he was feeling.

Jonathan looked at me with wet eyes. "I can't tell you how much all of this means to me. I don't understand why my mother was so secretive. This information is so valuable to me."

I was so happy at that moment – just to see Jonathan happy.

Chapter Twenty-Four – The Making of a Mystery

Perhaps the habit of intrigue is catching – in the air or the walls.
Like secret passages, only in the mind.
~Susan Kenney, "Garden of Malice"

There was more. Amongst all the photos and papers Jonathan had showed me were some old documents Jonathan had recently acquired from Heide. Heide's father (Richard's brother) had kept some letters he had received from Richard, along with a US diplomatic passport, issued to Richard in 1946, just eight months after World War II came to an end.

Heide had told us about her Uncle Richard being summoned to Washington, D.C. by President Truman to help with the plan for the Allied occupation's role in the reconstruction and restoration of post-war Europe. She didn't know too much about it, except that his work was related to the beginning of what would eventually become the *Marshall Plan* (officially the *European Recovery Program*, established in 1948), an American initiative to aid post Western Europe.

After Heide's father died, she found amongst his papers old carbon copies of correspondence between President Truman and Richard. The letters confirmed that Richard was appointed by Edwin Pauley, the American representative on the Allied Reparations Commission, to travel to Germany after

World War II to assist with reconstruction efforts. The letters were typewritten, and the carbon copy of one of the letters included handwritten notes, presumably written in Richard's own hand:

I had a nice visit with the President and got his instructions. –R

Also, in red ink and underlined: *Destroy this.*

I was impressed. My grandfather had a diplomatic passport and instructions directly from the President to travel to Germany, his home country, after World War II.

Even in the years before and during the War, Richard's engineering expertise led him to consult and work for the government. In the State of California alone, his pedigree was remarkable. In 1941, Richard had a residence in Sacramento and was working as Director of State Department of Natural Resources. By 1943, Richard had been appointed as the California State Railroad Commissioner. Census data showed that Richard maintained his home in Fallbrook, California, with his wife, Katherine and his two children, but he also had a residence in San Francisco. Jonathan was born in March of 1943 in Santa Barbara, California.

While this might help explain the secrecy, the false name on the birth certificate, and the sudden move to Santa Barbara just before Jonathan was born, Jonathan still questioned why his mother never shared with him any details about his father. And, why *Santa Barbara?* There was no record of other family members or any other connection to anyone or anything in Santa Barbara, but that is where Richard decided to tuck his pregnant mistress away so that she could give birth and raise their lovechild, alone.

And, why use the name *Carl Robert Winter* on Jonathan's birth records? The name *Carl Robert Winter* didn't have any connection to either Millie's side of the family or Richard's that we could readily identify. Were they trying to hide something more than just the affair and the illegitimate child? Richard was born in Germany, not San Francisco. Richard, of course, still had business and government connections and traveled often to the San Francisco and Washington, D.C. areas.

Richard's work during the time before and during World War II involved protecting California's infrastructure. The defense of the coastline, and in particular, the San Francisco Bay, as well as travel routes such as the railroads was of paramount importance during this time. Not only was there a large civilian population and interior agricultural industry to be protected, but there were major military and industrial complexes in the Bay Area, including a large explosives manufacturing plant, that were prime targets for a possible wartime attack.

Wartime was a scary time for everyone, especially for those Americans of Japanese, German, and Italian ancestry. After the attack on Pearl Harbor, President Roosevelt ordered the detainment of all individuals deemed to be "enemy aliens." Most affected, of course, were Japanese resident-aliens and Japanese-Americans, who, simply because of their Japanese ancestry, were thought to be potentially dangerous to American security.

The government's internment of Italian and German Americans, however, is a lesser known story. German and Italian Americans, considered to be of "enemy ancestry," were also viewed as potentially dangerous, particularly immigrants. The government enforced "alien enemy registration," individual and group exclusion from military zones, internee exchanges, deportation, repatriation, travel restrictions, and even property confiscation. The human cost of these civil liberties violations was high. Families were broken apart, reputations ruined, homes and belongings lost. By the end of the war, eleven thousand persons of German ancestry, including many American-born children, were interned. Scary stuff, if you happened to be of German ancestry.

Wartime for those of German ancestry in the US was daunting for other reasons, as well. The German-American *Bund*, established in 1936 as an organization of ethnic Germans living in the United States, promoted the pro-Nazi stance among German-born Americans as part of its program. *Bundists* developed a nationwide system of retreats, businesses, publications, and other propaganda in an attempt to promote a favorable view of Nazi Germany. The *Bund* also created its own versions of the Hitler Youth and SS squadrons (the Nazi special police force). The *Bund* lured German Americans to their "pro-American" rallies across the nation, where they displayed the Nazi insignia and handed out pins and badges promoting loyalty to the homeland and to the Nazi regime.

While the *Bund* was busy trying to rally and persuade German Americans toward Nazi-thinking, Nazi strategists – including the *Abwehr*, the German intelligence agency – began implementing their own covert operations and attempts at espionage by placing operatives in key American cities with orders to infiltrate big business, industries related to the war effort, and even local government. Operatives were charged with trying to persuade German-American citizens to join or assist in the Nazi cause.

Even before America ever fired a shot in World War II, the FBI had uncovered a massive ring of Nazi spies operating on U.S. soil. The thirty-three German agents who formed the Duquesne spy ring had infiltrated key jobs in the United States (mostly in and around the East Coast) to get information that could be used in the event of war and to carry out acts of sabotage.

Although not as well documented, there is evidence of yet another Nazi spy ring that operated from the West Coast down to Mexico through a deep-cover portal at El Paso, Texas. This sleeper cell was allegedly run by spymasters at the German consulate in San Francisco. The task of the agents and saboteurs was to obtain information about and slow down production at certain factories and within industries concerned with and supporting the American war effort. Only the inner circle of the Roosevelt White House and a few FBI agents were aware of the covert activities and the extent to which German agents had infiltrated American industry and local government in order to get close to industry leaders and influential politicians.

The German spymasters were actively searching for vulnerable Americans of German ancestry in key industry and government positions to recruit for their intelligence gathering efforts. They were not above seeking out individuals who might be persuaded through extortion or even harassment of family members to divulge secrets or participate in anti-American activities. Anyone of German ancestry with status or a position of importance or prominence in government or industry could be a target. Throughout the war, attempts were made to establish agents within the United States, including in California.

My grandfather, Richard, even though he was a naturalized U.S. citizen, was a full-blooded German. He came from Saxony to the United States at the turn of the twentieth century. He had extensive knowledge of natural resources and expertise in the fields of engineering, construction, and transportation. His peers and colleagues were titans of industry and government. This was all stuff that Nazi spies could have made good use of.

Millie, too, was of German heritage. She worked for years as a secretary in local government in Berkeley, California. For many years, she was personal secretary to Hollis Thompson, who was Berkeley's City Manager from 1930 to 1940. Her family had ties to the elite social society in the Bay Area. In fact, her German grandfather, William Lutkey, was the chief of the Oakland Fire Department for twenty years and served with the department from the horse-drawn days through the Great Depression and up to modern times, from 1901 to his retirement in 1947. His father, Millie's great grandfather, came from Hamburg, Germany to the United States as a small boy and eventually found his way to Northern California during the Gold Rush days in the mid-1800s. He eventually settled in Oakland, California and is considered one of Oakland's founding Pioneers.

It's unclear exactly how and when Richard and Millie met, but it is clear they were carrying on their affair in the early 1940s in the Bay Area. There is no hard evidence that Richard and Millie were hiding from the threat of internment when they moved pregnant Millie to Santa Barbara, or that they were being harassed by Nazi spies that may have been skulking around in their professional or social circles, but it's certainly plausible that the move to Santa Barbara and the false name used on Jonathan's birth certificate were both meant to distance the well-heeled German-Americans from the reach of any Nazis who might have had their sights set on Richard or his family. Knowledge of an extramarital affair and a bastard child might be the perfect fodder for blackmail or extortion efforts in exchange for valuable intelligence.

Jonathan and I agreed that there was certainly a possibility that Richard and Millie wanted to get Jonathan as far away from the reach of the big city buzz and war efforts as possible.

Apparently, however, according to government records and reports, the Nazi spies who were lurking around on the West Coast were, for the most part, unskilled and amateurish. While there was quite a bit of activity on the East Coast (the arrest and conviction of the thirty-three spies who made up the Duquesne Spy Ring is just one example) efforts to infiltrate the West Coast and do any real damage or gather any valuable information never panned out.

Bungling spies. Thank goodness. California was left basically unscathed during the War. Millie and her new little baby, Jonathan, were safely tucked away in the beautiful seaside town of Santa Barbara, California – miles away from the bustling activity and intrigue in the Bay Area.

Richard eventually married Millie, but that didn't happen until 1949. Ann and I have been unable to find any records of Richard's divorce from his first wife, Katherine (another possible scandal and reason for the secrecy?). Then, just one month after Richard and Millie were married, Richard died. He had suffered a stroke in 1947 and had never fully recovered.

He was sixty-seven years old. Jonathan was only six.

Jonathan doesn't recall a time when Richard lived at home with him and Millie. He does recall a time when his father was visiting their home in Santa Barbara and they were spending some quiet time together. Jonathan remembers that it was very low key – it was after Richard's stroke and they spent most of their time together sitting on a couch at home. Millie must have snapped a photo of the two of them together. Jonathan still has the black and white image. It is a photo he cherishes, as it is the only picture he has of the two of them together. Jonathan was just a small boy, but he remembers clearly his father talking to him about the perils of war.

"War is bad," he can remember his father saying. "You must avoid war at all costs." Jonathan has carried this sentiment with him his entire life.

After poring over documents and pictures and telling stories, we settled in for dinner. We enjoyed some roasted salmon caught locally by Phil with a blueberry sauce and the fresh greens Jonathan and I found at the farmers' market. Megan also cooked some shrimp and used some of the seasoning I brought from home to flavor the butter. After dinner, Leona serenaded us with her version of "Let it Go." She's a good little singer.

Before I left for the evening, Jonathan and I made plans to get together in the morning to just sit and talk and get to know each other. It would be Easter Sunday, and Phil, Megan, and Leona would be gone for the morning and the early part of the afternoon at a friend's house for brunch and an Easter egg hunt, so Jonathan and I would have time to just be alone and talk.

As I drove myself back to the hotel, I caught myself smiling at the thought of my new family. My heart was full of pride for Jonathan and all he had accomplished in his life. I was proud of my father. And, I had helped him to discover the story of his own father – my grandfather! I had a strange sense of accomplishment – like I had completed a task, even though in reality the task of getting to know these people – my family, my tribe – had just begun.

Chapter Twenty-Five – Keeping It Simple

People who pride themselves on their "complexity" and deride others for being "simplistic" should realize that the truth is often not very complicated. What gets complex is evading the truth.
~Thomas Sowell

I slept well and woke up with a sort of momentum that pushed me to move forward without effort. I'm not usually a morning person, but on that particular morning, I felt weightless as I glided to the bathroom to get myself ready for the day ahead.

I arrived at Jonathan's home and knocked on the front door. He surprised me by appearing at the side of the house near the porch. He was wearing a dirty, white apron and wielding a large butcher knife. I was reminded of my adopted dad, who loved to cook and could be found often in our kitchen working with one of his favored German Henckels knives.

"Hello, kiddo! C'mon back!" He motioned with the knife for me to come around. We were skipping the main house this morning and going directly to the part of the property that he called home – the small, detached, converted garage beside the house.

The tiny building looked more like a hunting cabin that belonged deep in the woods. The inside space was no larger than a studio apartment. There was just one main room with a kitchen area and window along one wall, a bathroom in a far corner, and a futon for sitting and sleeping against another wall. Jonathan's computer was near the door, sitting atop a large desk that was piled high with stacks of paper, magazines and books. The floors were unfinished wood, dark with age, with several thick old rugs placed in strategic places.

"Make yourself at home. I even tidied up a little bit for you." Jonathan chuckled.

Jonathan went back to the task at hand. He stood at the kitchen sink, busying himself with prepping several lamb shanks for our Easter dinner. The metallic smell of blood and bones hung in the air. In our email conversations over the last year, we had talked about our shared love for lamb and how we both enjoy cooking. I was touched that he remembered and delighted that he was preparing a meal for me.

As I watched Jonathan working, I considered my surroundings – a glimpse into the world of my father.

The living space was masculine, slightly cluttered but neat, with a creative energy. The room was not so much purposefully decorated, but it was full of items that were obviously meaningful to Jonathan. Handmade shelves and bookcases were stuffed with books, primitive art, unusual artifacts, and simple items from nature – like interesting rocks and pine cones. There were old parts – I could only guess radio parts – and other old electronics, rusty metal things, a Native American basket or two, a set of tiny leather moccasins, and a few carved wooden figurines. I noticed a large, clear glass item sitting on a table near the door. It was thick and heavy, curved – like a big shallow bowl – but it didn't seem to have a purpose. I asked Jonathan what it was and where it came from. He said it was an old lens of some sort. He couldn't remember where he got it, but he liked its shape and the smoothness of the glass, so he kept it.

As I wandered through the room, touching some of the items that interested me, I thought of the jars of treasures I keep in the cupboards above the closets in my sons' bedrooms.

When my boys were little, as they romped and tumbled through their childhood days, they would pick up what I thought were peculiar odds and ends – trash, really – like feathers, rocks, old washers, bottle caps, and stuff them into the pockets of their little jeans. At the end of each week, I would dig into the tiny pockets before doing laundry and toss the found treasures into big mason jars for safekeeping. Why did I save all those absurd bits of debris? I'm sure my boys, now grown, have all but forgotten those treasures gathered so long ago. I still have those jars, filled with those valuable childhood memories. Someday, I'll hand the treasure-filled jars over to their rightful owners.

I shared the story of the treasure-filled mason jars with Jonathan. He laughed and made some comment about wondering what the boys would think of those treasures now.

Here in Jonathan's tiny abode, amid what seemed like a profusion of unrelated, yet interesting objects, the room made sense. I felt at home.

On the top shelf in one corner of the tiny apartment, I noticed two drones with cameras attached. I was a little surprised at this, as Jonathan didn't strike me as a drone sort of person. I asked him about them. He told me he was fascinated with the technology, and he enjoyed flying the drones over his property and into the woods for a new perspective. Ah… the technology, of course. If technology can expand an artist's view of the world around him, why not embrace it?

I sat on the futon and got to know Jonathan's cat, Mitch. Mitch looked like he could have been related to my tabby family at home. I scratched the top of his head, and he rubbed my legs in appreciation while his tail whipped at my ankles. He was friendly and calm and seemed content to stay inside, even with the door of the tiny cabin left wide open to the big beautiful world outside. My cats would have bolted, eager to hunt and explore in the great wilderness just outside the door.

We eventually walked over to the kitchen in the big house so that Jonathan could get the lamb shanks in the oven for their slow braise. Once the meaty bones were in the oven, Jonathan walked me back outside. He wanted to show me his studio. I was excited to finally get to see where all of Jonathan's artistic ideas came to life.

We descended the concrete steps into the workshop. The space was originally a basement or cellar – windowless, cold and dark. Jonathan flipped a switch at the bottom of the steps and there was light. The smell was musty, but not unpleasant. The shelves on either side of the small space were piled with sheets and coils of raw materials, including precious metals – copper, bronze, bright sterling wire. There were several large machines lurking in the shadows – automated devices for working the metal or the stones, I presumed. The workshop seemed cramped to me, but I could tell that the space, with its clutter and tangle of tools was meaningful to Jonathan. The bench in the center was piled with an assortment of objects: a half-finished mask, pieces of flattened and formed metal, colorful unpolished stones, and an old rusty coffee can stuffed with small utensils and implements. Amid the supplies and tools and the singular stool, three bright bulbs hung over the workbench in strategic places from plain cords.

How could the intricate beauty and brilliance I saw in Jonathan's art and jewelry come from such chaos and disorder? Such is the life of an artist. I was beginning to understand how the artist sees things in order to create his art. I took it in and held it close to my heart. It is part of me, after all.

The rest of the day and evening was casual and easy. Before Megan and the rest of the family arrived home, Jonathan and I talked and looked at some of the documents and pictures again. We bounced around some *what ifs?* and *whys?* that neither one of us could answer.

Why does Jonathan have no memory of Margaret?

Why won't Margaret acknowledge us?

Why was Jonathan's mother so secretive about Jonathan's father, even later in life, when the secret was no longer a threat?

Why did Jonathan's father use a false name on Jonathan's birth certificate, in effect giving Jonathan a false name?

Were Jonathan's parents (my grandparents) hiding more than just their affair?

Why would Jonathan's mother want to hide the rich history and legacy of his father's life and his contributions to society?

Was there something more to be revealed to both of us?

It is, of course, human nature to question our surroundings, our purpose, and our very being. It is because we have these questions that human life is so deeply satisfying at one moment and so deeply troubling the next. Apparently, it's not enough just to *be*. Just to accept who we are and where we end up in life. Jonathan and I were both still curious about so much.

But, I *do* want to live in the moment. Experience the now and enjoy it. Appreciate it. I *am* living *physically* in this very moment, but you know how it works. Thoughts wander. And, nearly all our thoughts revolve around the past or the future, don't they? The thoughts of a child will often be focused on the events that will take place in the future – no matter if these are upcoming events in the next moments (*What will happen if I don't do my homework?*) or situations that lie many years in the future (*What do I want to be when I grow up?*). Our elders, however, often focus on situations from the past, with thoughts revolving around the things that have already happened – the *good old days*. Young or old, we want to make sense of it. We can't help it. Questions, questions, and more questions.

I must keep reminding myself: *not all questions have an answer*.

The rest of the clan came home in the early afternoon. Leona proudly showed off the goodies in her Easter basket. I blew up a balloon for her and we played a fierce game of slow-motion balloon volleyball in the living room. Leona made up her own rules, and I was happy to abide by them. She won, of course.

Megan opened a bottle of wine, and Jonathan popped open a Corona for himself. When we finally sat down to dinner, I was feeling the family spirit. I was comfortable and content. I was also impressed. Jonathan had made a red wine reduction sauce with the pan drippings from the lamb. Lamb is one of my favorites and a treat I rarely get at home because my husband doesn't eat meat. I couldn't stop swooning about the lamb shanks. Megan made some rice and a salad to bring it all together. Dinner at the family table was warm and wonderful.

Chapter Twenty-Six – Three Words

No person is your friend who demands your silence,
or denies your right to grow.
~Alice Walker

Sunday night was my last night in Bellingham. Back at the hotel, even with my heart and head so full of intriguing newness – new personalities, stories, family history, dreams about the past, and hopes of the future – I slept well. I awoke Monday morning once again with a purpose and no desire to linger in bed. I had promised Jonathan I would come by to say goodbye before hitting the road to Seattle. I packed up my things, dragged my suitcase to the car, and slipped back inside the hotel to grab some yogurt and coffee in the lobby-turned-free-breakfast-buffet.

Before driving to Jonathan's house, I took a short detour to Bellingham Bay. I wanted to see for myself where the forest met the sea in this enchanted place.

Bellingham is situated in Whatcom County. Whatcom is the most northwestern county in the contiguous United States, just twenty miles from the Canadian border.

I drove west, knowing I'd reach the water in short order. Before long, I emerged from a winding, forest-lined highway into a clearing that opened into a large marina. I parked and walked to the water's edge. The marina was full of pleasure boats large and small, tied to their moorings, bobbing gently. It was Monday, so there weren't many people milling around the docks. The boats were mostly empty and sat peacefully, proudly resting in their aquatic cradles, waiting patiently for the next weekend or holiday when they'd be geared up and once again taken out to sea. I took a few photos. The day was bright and brisk. I was amused to see the small mounds of colorful tulips blooming all around.

Just southeast of Bellingham is Skagit County, which hosts the Skagit Valley Tulip Festival each spring. Each year, hundreds of thousands of people head to Skagit Valley to enjoy the celebration of spring as the tulip fields burst into bloom. The tulip fields are the crops of commercial growers which have been in the region for over fifty years. Luckily for me, there are tulips all over nearby Whatcom County, too. Even there in the marina.

But, it wasn't the tulips that drew me. Like Jonathan, I've always been drawn to the water. Jonathan was lucky enough to be born in the quaint and beautiful seaside town of Santa Barbara, rich with history and miles of picturesque beaches. When he relocated to Washington, he told me that choosing Bellingham with his wife, Judith, had a lot to do with being near the water. Even though I was born inland in California, I have always looked to the ocean for a sense of calm and clarity. It's grounding in a strange way because, for me, it's about forgetting the earth we stand on, with its stresses and complications. It's about mentally floating away from the personal anxieties, allowing the waves and the pull of the tide to wash away details and allowing a stronger focus on what is in front of me. A sort of existential experience that delivers focus and lucidity.

What was in front of me at this moment was the revelation of a new family; a new beginning. It felt like I had found part of what I had been looking for, but I was keenly aware that my journey wasn't over.

How did I get to know and bond with a new family at my age? I had family on the adoptive side I had difficulty just keeping in touch with. And, there was my immediate family. It was going to be difficult for them to recognize my new family as "family." They hadn't met them, and while they supported my journey, it wasn't something they sought. I wanted my sons to get to know Jonathan and his family and learn about their grandfather's colorful and accomplished life. But, I hadn't been able to get their attention. I was hoping their curiosity would expand as they grew into adulthood. In the meanwhile, I was coming to terms with the fact that it was a solitary journey I was on.

On the one hand, I was elated about finding Jonathan, Megan, Leona, and Phil, and I could not have been treated better by them. They were so open and welcoming to me. What more could I ask for?

But, how did I hold on to it? How did I meld this new family with my "old" one?

Perhaps I shouldn't have worried about the melding. My goal was and is still to be open, communicate, and learn as much as I can. Jonathan's family (my paternal family) was open to knowing and learning, so my goal should have been to simply keep the lines of communication, as well as my heart and soul, open.

I got back into my rental car and headed inland towards Jonathan's house. It was time to say goodbye for the time being. The drive to Jonathan's house was short. I knew my way now without the GPS. As I pulled into the driveway, I could see the door to Jonathan's little flat in the back was open. I went straight back and found him on the computer. We hugged and sat for a few moments, just reviewing all the revelations we had discovered together. He was so pleased to have learned so much about his father. He told me over and over that he felt like a different person. I knew exactly how he felt.

Jonathan expressed some interest in knowing more about his mother, Millie, and I promised I would do my best to do some sleuthing and get back to him. I, too, wanted to learn more about the strong, but secretive woman. I believe Jonathan thought of her as more of a stern, taciturn figure. Both of us wanted to know what was behind the stony exterior. Fear? Humility? Or, was she guarding herself and her son against something else? Secrets she could not (or would not) share.

Jonathan walked me to my car. We promised to stay in touch and to keep sharing. We hugged again. I thanked him for everything. We were both smiling. His was a familiar smile now. I opened the car door and stood for a moment watching Jonathan walk away.

"Bye!" I called out, as I ducked into the driver's seat.

"Bye!" he called back. And, then, "I love you!"

What? I looked up, but he had already rounded the corner. It felt weird to holler back, "I love you, too!" but I did anyway.

Epilogue

Truth, like gold, is to be obtained not by its growth,
but by washing away from it all that is not gold.
~Leo Tolstoy

It has been over three years since I met my biological father, Jonathan, my sister, Megan, and her family. It's an easy relationship, albeit complicated, as most long-distance relationships tend to be. We usually email each other several times a month. Sometimes, we Skype, although that happens less and less now. I understand my father. He's an elusive one – he doesn't like social media, the immediacy of the cell phone, and he's not fond of computers. He's happy to keep his world small. But, he also fully understands that without that DNA test, computers, and social media, his small world would still be in the shadows, and he'd be confined by the unknown.

The same is true for me. I now live in the light. I know fully who I am and where I came from. Still, I have never met my biological mother, nor have I ever spoken to her. I'm okay with that. I have gotten to know two of her siblings, my two aunts, who have helped me understand that it's okay if someone else's terms of forgiveness are different than what you had in mind. And, sometimes simply leaving something (or someone) behind is what can heal you.

My brother, Tom, has had a recent change of heart about finding his biological family. I've been helping him track down clues. DNA would be a great help to us, but there is, apparently, something wrong with his spit. His DNA failed. Twice. It's odd… and rare. We tease him that it means he's got alien DNA in him. This was the explanation from *23andMe*:

> *If necessary, the lab will make multiple attempts at all stages of the process in order to provide results; however, due to biological variability some people simply don't have a high enough concentration of DNA in their saliva for our technology to process.*

He's considering submitting his saliva to a different company. In the meantime, we soldier on with what little information we have. We've had some encouraging leads, and we've also hit some dead ends. I keep telling him we'll get to the truth somehow. I know we will.

My boys are twenty-six (Zach) and eighteen (Garrett). It's unfathomable to me how quickly they've become adults. I have much to be thankful for when it comes to my boys. They have friends, girlfriends, interests, ambitions, and meet most challenges with poise and competence. They are thoughtful and empathetic. They humor their mother and keep in touch.

Guy and I have been married now for over twenty years. He's preparing for retirement in a year or so. Who knows what we'll do or where we'll end up after his retirement. I keep pushing for a move to Coastal Washington, to be closer to Jonathan. I would like to get to know him better.

###

Ersatz Life
(part two)
A poem by Laureen Pittman

She nurtures the trust
She has in herself and accepts
The Truth will be revealed
Quietly, as in a dream, without fanfare
Or like a tempest, with a chaos
Of emotion.

A journey exhilarating and daunting
As the Truth settles
into the cracks of her soul.
Her heart begins to know
      Wholeness
      Heritage
      Family

Acknowledgements

I'd like to acknowledge the people who have given their time, effort, advice, and support to me during my journey. You all deserve to be acknowledged for it. I ask forgiveness of all those who have been with me over the years and whose names I fail to mention below. If you are a part of my life, you have been a part of this crazy and emotional journey, and for that, I thank you.

First, thank you to my *Willies*, who know me better than I know myself. You listened to me rant and cry and tell my story at various times throughout my journey. You were all so helpful with your encouragement and guidance with the early direction of this book.

Thank you to my early readers, including Christine Larsen, Teresa Rhyne, Barbara Shackleton, and Michelle Oulette, who each gave useful, constructive feedback on my book.

Next, thanks to my friend, Lisa Hjulberg, who is also adopted, and whose encouragement and insight helped me feel validated with the strong feelings (and sometimes the lack thereof) about being adopted and what, if anything, we should *do* about it.

Thank you to another dear friend, Nancy "Ann" Teixeira, who, out of friendship and the goodness of her own heart, spent hours of her time using her amazing research skills to help me figure out *my* genealogy. Nancy made it possible for me and Jonathan to discover and embrace the rich history that lives in our blood and a legacy we would have never known. I also want to thank Nancy for always being there for me, for providing invaluable suggestions and guidance, and for allowing me to bounce off weird and abstract theories about the complicated puzzle that is my unique family. She helped make sense of all of it.

A big thank you to readers and followers of my blog, *Adoption: My Truth* (www.adoptionmytruth.com), many of whom are part of the adoption community. Your comments and encouragement kept me searching, discovering, and sharing.

Thank you to Christine Koubek and Heather Katz, co-founders of the website and on-line community, *Secret Sons & Daughters*, which gives adoptees the opportunity to tell their stories. Christine and Heather are champions of the adopted, promoting and fostering a deeper understanding of what it means to be adopted through the power of stories. I appreciate the opportunity they gave to me to share part of my story through *Secret Sons & Daughters*.

Thank you to Lydia and Robertsen Ashman, for their artistic, collaborative eye and for bringing my vision for my cover art to life in a beautiful and meaningful way.

Thanks to my Inland Empire writing family, especially Robert and Leila Kirkconnell and Angie Martin, all of whom provided support and encouragement throughout the writing and publishing process. I could not have completed the writing of this book without Angie's wizardry.

Above all I want to thank my husband, Guy, and my boys, Zach and Garrett, who supported and encouraged me throughout this journey, in spite of the fact that I was, undoubtedly, anxious and surly at times, and for being understanding for all the time the project took me away from them.

About Laureen Pittman

Laureen started blogging about her adoption journey in 2013 (adoptionmytruth.com). As her own story evolved, she realized that there was a much larger truth that needed to be explored and shared. She wanted to bring her story to life—not just for herself and her family, but for other adoptees who yearn to learn their own truths and for families touched by adoption who want to understand and value the heart and soul of an adoptee. Laureen's writing has also been published on the blog, Secret Sons and Daughters – Adoptee Tales From the Sealed Records Era.

Laureen lives in sunny Southern California with her husband, two sons, and three cats. She is a paralegal by profession and worked for lawyers and law firms large and small for over 20 years after graduating from college with a Bachelor of Arts in Political Science. When she's not writing or cat-herding, she's usually barefoot and in the kitchen (because she hates wearing shoes and she loves cooking).

Made in the USA
Columbia, SC
24 December 2019